HISTORIC AMERICA

THE SOUTH

HISTORIC AMERICA
THE SOUTH

BROOKS ROBARDS

THUNDER BAY
P·R·E·S·S
SAN DIEGO, CALIFORNIA

Acknowledgments and Photo Credits

The publisher would like to thank all those who assisted in the production of this book, including those listed at right, and: Lone Nerup Sorensen for the gazetteer and index; Paula Reel for illustration. Grateful acknowledgment is also made to the following individuals and institutions for permission to reproduce illustrations and photographs: © **Tony Arruza**: 7, 10–11, 12, 13, 14–15, 16–17, 18–19, 21, 22, 24–5, 27, 29, 31, 32, 33, 36–7, 40–1, 44–5, 52–3, 60–1, 64, 68–9, 72, 73, 76–7, 88–9, 97, 100, 101, 104–5, 108–9, 116–7, 120, 121, 124–5, 128; **Collection of Glenn and Lorraine Myers**: 44; © **A. Blake Gardner**: 112; **Hays T. Watkins Research Library, Baltimore & Ohio Railroad Museum**: 111; © **Rudi Holnsteiner**: 113; © **Balthazar Korab**: 20, 30; **Library of Congress, Historic American Buildings Survey Collection**: 98, 99, 102b, 106t, 106b, 107, 110 both, 118, 119, 126; **Prints and Photographs Division**: 35, 43, 46, 47, 50, 51 (both), 54, 55, 56, 57, 63, 75b, 79, 84, 85b, 87, 92, 94, 95, 102t, 114, 115, 125 both, 127; **Serials and Government Publications Division**: 70r; **National Archives**: 62, 67, 70l, 74, 75, 76, 78, 83, 86, 90, 91, 96, 103, 122, 123; **The National Archives, Public Record Office, Kew (UK)**: 58–9; © **Rod Patterson**: 6, 26; © **Paula Reel**: 38, 39; © **Michael A. Smith**: 85t; © **Graeme Teague**: 1, 2, 4, 8–9, 28, 48, 49, 65, 80, 81; **U.S. Department of the Interior, National Park Service Division**: Richard Frear: 93; **The Yale University Map Collection, photograph © Joseph Szaszfai**: 71

Thunder Bay Press

An imprint of the Advantage Publishers Group
5880 Oberlin Drive, San Diego, CA 92121-4794
www.thunderbaybooks.com

All notations of errors or omissions should be addressed to Thunder Bay Press, editorial department, at the above address. All other correspondence (author inquiries, permissions) concerning the content of this book should be addressed to Saraband, The Arthouse, 752–756 Argyle Street, Glasgow G3 8UJ, Scotland (hermes@saraband.net).

ISBN 1-57145-985-5

Library of Congress Cataloging-in-Publication Data available upon request.

Printed in China

1 2 3 4 5 07 06 05 04 03

Above, left: This Art Deco lifeguard hut is a colorful landmark on Miami Beach, Florida.

Page 1: A decorative balustrade with trelliswork, typical of many historic Southern homes.

Page 2: This ruined home on Georgia's Cumberland Island evokes the spirit of *Gone With the Wind.*

SERIES EDITOR: John S. Bowman
EDITORS: Sara Hunt and Deborah Hayes
PHOTOGRAPHY: Tony Arruza and Graeme Teague
ART DIRECTOR: Nikki L. Fesak

TABLE OF CONTENTS

Introduction

THE SOUTH

8

The South might be called America's most romantic region. With its mild climate and leisurely pace, the region evokes the atmosphere of a much-storied, earlier era. In that view of history, aristocratic Southerners enjoyed a genteel lifestyle, with ladies in long, hooped dresses and gentlemen sipping mint juleps on the porches of handsome Southern plantations.

Whether or not this interpretation of history is accurate or representative, the fact remains that the South can claim the distinction of being the oldest settled region in the nation. St. Augustine, Florida, was founded in 1565 by Spaniard Pedro Menéndez de Avilés. The Spanish were moving through the Southwest by then, but they didn't establish their first colony there—in New Mexico—until 1598. Jamestown, Virginia, the nation's oldest British settlement, dates back to 1607, while Plymouth, Massachusetts, did not come into existence until 1620.

Historically speaking, the South is usually identified as consisting of those states that seceded from the Union in 1861 to form the Confederacy. Texas also seceded, but with its cultural elements of the "Old West," that state seems better placed in the Southwest, which has its own volume in this series. Both Maryland—one of the original thirteen colonies—and Kentucky are frequently described as border states, because many residents of the two states felt strong sympathies for the Confederacy. Although Kentucky did not secede, it still traditionally belongs in the South. Maryland fits more readily in the Mid-Atlantic region, as does Washington, DC. We have included twelve states in this historical survey of the region:

Page 6: The historic Caldwell Place Barn is located in Cataloochee Valley, Tennessee, which was at one time one of the most successful farming communities in the Great Smoky Mountains. Remnants of the region's pioneer farming days remain there to this day.

Page 7: This great egret was photographed at Bear Island in South Carolina. The Bear Island Wildlife Management Area in Colleton County features many wading birds, eagles, and song birds.

Overleaf: New River Wilderness, part of Apalachicola National Forest, is located in Florida's panhandle. Also known as Mud Swamp Wilderness, it is swampy, wet, and densely covered with titi and slash pines.

Left: Sunset on Key Biscayne in Florida is one of many tourist attractions of this resort town. Explorer Juan Ponce de Leon claimed the island for Spain in 1513 and named it Santa Marta.

Above: The barn building pictured is part of the Elijah Oliver homestead at Cades Cove in Great Smoky Mountains National Park. The area was first opened to settlement in 1819, after the land was acquired from the Cherokee.

Opposite: This aerial view shows Fort Jefferson on Garden Key and nearby Bush Key in Florida, two islands in the Dry Tortugas—so named by Ponce de Leon for the dry sea tortoise meat found there. A lighthouse was first built on Garden Key in 1825.

Alabama, Arkansas, Florida, Georgia, Kentucky, Louisiana, Mississippi, North Carolina, South Carolina, Tennessee, Virginia, and West Virginia.

Early in the history of the South, a number of European nations vied for control of this part of the New World. The Spanish, already established in the Caribbean and Middle America, built forts and missions primarily along the coast, particularly in Florida but as far north as Virginia. Many of the South's early monuments consist of the remains of these Spanish forts and missions. French explorers in the South focused more on the Mississippi River Valley. New Orleans, Louisiana, continues to exhibit the influence of the French on its cultural traditions and dialects. The British colonized the most aggressively in the South, beginning with Jamestown, and by the end of the Seven Years War in Europe in 1763, Britain had become the dominant colonial empire.

In the Tidewater section of Virginia, people still speak in a dialect more British than American.

The Southern drawl, famous for its "y'all" (you-all), distinguishes the region's speech, although in fact dialects vary to some degree by state. Linguists point out that Southern speech has been strongly influenced by French, as a result of France's ownership of the Louisiana Territory, and by the African languages brought over by slaves. "Southspeak" is a richly nuanced and melodious version of American English.

Southern hospitality—that general warmth and receptiveness for which the region is famous—may have originated in the South's agrarian social structure. Since early Southerners did not live in close proximity to each other, when visitors arrived, they usually stayed awhile, and it was time to feast. Today, as part of the Sun Belt—that economic division of the United States stretching

Right: *Sunrise is a special event on Nanny Goat Beach at Sapelo Island, Georgia. Loggerhead sea turtles, an endangered species, come ashore there to lay their eggs.*

from Florida to California—the South has left behind what can be called its slow-paced, backward-looking image and become a vibrant, industrially thriving region. Yet the notion of a more courtly way of life lingers.

From a geographic perspective, the coastal South is part of a 300-mile-wide plain that runs north-south from New York Harbor down through Virginia, North and South Carolina, and Georgia. From there, this plain continues around Florida to Alabama, Mississippi, and Louisiana along the Gulf of Mexico. Brackish tidal water extends into the bays of Virginia and North Carolina as far south as Cape Hatteras in this section of the South. Tobacco farming there in the seventeenth and eighteenth centuries led to elimination of the region's original hardwood forests and a pattern of serious soil erosion. Early farmers in the South were not cognizant of the importance of soil conservation. They believed when the soil stopped producing, they could move on to new fields.

The South's coastline has some of the most beautiful and tourist-friendly beaches in the nation. Cape Hatteras is the first of a series of prominent capes, including Cape Lookout, Cape Fear, and Cape Romain, along the coasts of North and South Carolina. Then the coast features sea islands off Georgia, South Carolina, and northern Florida. As the earth's ice caps have melted, sea level has risen an average of six inches per century along the South's coast, changing its appearance considerably. The tidal flats of South Carolina and Georgia have made those areas attractive for rice crops. Florida is, in fact, a peninsula, with long sandy beaches to the east, coral beaches at the southern-

most tip, and more irregular ones on the western side. The Gulf Coast section of the South features barrier beaches and lagoons. The South's coastal climate is mild, but the area is often hit by hurricanes.

Inland from the South's coastal section is the hilly Piedmont Plateau, with elevations from 500 to 1,000 feet. Southern soils in the Piedmont—"foot of the mountain"—tend to a red or yellow clay base. Beyond the range of the last round of glaciation, the Piedmont has weathered rocks and old soil. A series of rivers draining from the Appalachian Mountains crisscross the region and have encouraged construction of canals like the Susquehanna and Tidewater, built in 1840. Cotton thrived in the Piedmont Plateau but its intensive production has caused massive erosion and sedimentation of the land.

West of the Piedmont Plateau, the picturesque Blue Ridge Province of the Appalachians rises as high as 6,684 feet at Mount Mitchell in North Carolina's Blue Ridge Mountains. Tennessee's Ducktown Copper Basin produced copper smelts there that destroyed the natural vegetation, caused erosion, and has led to a badlands topography. West Virginia's plenteous coal deposits come from the carbonized remains of giant ferns that once grew in the Paleozoic era. Early mining techniques succeeded in destroying the environment of that part of West Virginia, creating spoil heaps and toxic streams. Today's surface mining is less destructive. The discovery of extensive salt brine deposits from fossilized Paleozoic seawater led to the development of Southern salt mines on the Kanawha River in West Virginia, and at Saltville, Virginia.

Left: *Water cascades down Linville Falls, a tourist attraction near Grandfather Mountain in North Carolina. Nearby Linville Gorge is known as North Carolina's Grand Canyon.*

Overleaf: *Laden with ripe fruit, this apple orchard is located near Cosby, Tennessee. Gatlinburg, Pigeon Forge, and Great Smoky Mountains National Park are near this peaceful country town once known as the "Moonshine Capital of the World."*

Above: *Lacy wrought-iron balconies reveal a French-Creole influence on the architecture of Elmscourt in Natchez, Mississippi. The Greek Revival home was originally owned by Ayers Merrill and is now listed on the National Registry of Historical Places.*

West of the Blue Ridge Province is the Appalachian Plateau, a major barrier to westward expansion in the South. This rugged section of the region reaches plateau heights of 4,000 feet. Oak trees create dense forests there, and clouds and fog predominate. King George III of Britain tried to stop the colonists' westward expansion by issuing the Proclamation of 1763, forbidding them to settle west of the Appalachians. The Proclamation proved unenforceable, and settlers poured into the Mississippi River Valley despite it.

The next geologic section of the South is known as the Interior Low Plateaus, and they stretch from the Appalachian Plateau to the Mississippi River Valley. Two of the prime areas here are the Kentucky Bluegrass Basin and the Nashville Basin in Tennessee, with some of the nation's richest soils. In contrast, the nearby highlands have poor soil. Limestone-created sinkholes and caves characterize the Interior Low and neighboring Ozark Plateaus.

Kentucky's Mammoth Cave is the world's largest cave system at 340 miles long, as currently surveyed. North of Bowling Green, Mammoth Cave became a national park in 1941 and has twelve miles of accessible trails with underground lakes, rivers, and waterfalls. Adjacent to the Interior Low and Ozark Plateaus is the Ouachita Province, featuring coal and bauxite (used in aluminum) deposits.

The Mississippi River Valley, consisting of parts of Arkansas, Tennessee, Mississippi, and Louisiana, makes up a geographically distinct section of the South. The giant Mississippi River, draining some 40 percent of the nation's watershed, has carried much erosional silt over the centuries and has been flood prone. No description of the South would be complete without a discussion of its rivers. The Mississippi is, of course, its largest, but other important rivers include the Ohio, which separates the western states of the South from the rest of the region. Emptying into the Atlantic are the Potomac, the Roanoake, the Cape Fear, the Santee, and the Savannah. Flowing into the Gulf of Mexico in addition to the Mississippi are the Sabine, the Red, the Tombigbee, the Alabama, and the Chattahoochee Rivers.

Plant life in the South is lush and prolific. Influenced by the ocean climate of the coast, it is sparse only along its sandy beaches, which attract tourists and water sports enthusiasts. The low, flat Tidewater section of Virginia is swampy, but the Great Dismal Swamp, running from Norfolk into North Carolina, is thick with forests. The northern section of Virginia borders the Chesapeake Bay—the nation's largest

Below: Middle Saluda River flows entirely within Jones Gap State Park in South Carolina. A trout stream, it was the first river protected by the state's Scenic Rivers Program.

estuary—an area mild in climate with "fair meadows and goodly tall trees," as one seventeenth-century visitor put it. Pine, oak, ash, and walnut grew in the days of European settlement, and tobacco and maize grew wild then in the state's grasslands.

Mountainous West Virginia, which began as part of Virginia, is heavily forested with pine, spruce, hemlock, maple, beech, cherry, hickory, and birch. It does not have a receptive terrain for farming, and much of it has become national forest. Included are the Monongahela, George Washington, and Jefferson National Forests. Some of the nation's largest trees, such as the world's tallest giant sycamore near Webster Springs, grow in West Virginia. The Mingo Oak, once America's largest white oak and possibly the world's largest, was almost 600 years old and 145 feet tall before it died in 1938. A number of rare plants grow in West Virginia, like the sundew, which devours insects; the phymosia; the box huckleberry—the world's oldest plant according to some botanists—and the prickly pear.

Nearby Kentucky has more rivers than any other state save Alaska, making white-water rafting a particularly popular sport there. Along its riverbanks grows the Kentucky Coffee Tree, the seeds of which were brewed by settlers to make a drink similar to java. The bluegrass after which the state is named was actually imported from England, probably by accident in livestock feed, during the seventeenth century.

The Appalachian Mountains create Tennessee's eastern border. Hickory, oak, and pine forests—to name a few of the major varieties—cover half the state.

Tennessee is touted as having the most diverse flora in North America. In adjacent North Carolina, with more coastal plains and cypress swamps, black gum trees inhabit the section of the Great Dismal Swamp that extends from Virginia into the northern part of the state. Pine forests dot the coastal plains. The grassy prairies of North Carolina's savanna extend inland beyond the coast. The Fall Line, demarcating geographic regions, creates the border between the state's plains country and the Piedmont hills west of it, where clay turns the soil red. Almost a dozen insect-eating plants, such as the Venus flytrap, inhabit Croatan National Forest. An Asian vine, called kudzu, has proliferated in North Carolina. It was imported to the South in the 1870s and has invaded so much of the region that it is now called the Scourge of the South. In North Carolina's Piedmont grow sourwood, sycamore, hemlock, oak, red spruce, and hickory trees.

The pine forests found in North Carolina's coastal plains also grow in South Carolina in an area called the Pine Barrens. At 500,000 acres, South Carolina vies with Louisiana for the most swampland in the United States, and like North Carolina, it has cypress trees in its wetlands and oaks, palmettos, and loblolly pines inland. What distinguishes so many Southern oaks and other trees is the Spanish moss that hangs from their branches.

Georgia is best known for its magnolia trees, but its 24 million acres of forest also have pine, cedar, elm, sycamore, poplar, palm, red maple, cypress, willow, hickory, gum, hemlock, and dogwood as well. In 1991, Brunswick, Georgia's fine sixty-two-foot cabbage

Opposite: *This hardwood forest grows in the upper Combahee River region of South Carolina's coastal lowlands. Boats traveled the Combahee in the eighteenth century en route to and from Charleston.*

Overleaf: *When settlers cleared the land at Providence Canyon State Park near Lumpkin, Georgia, less than 150 years ago for farming, erosion rapidly washed away the soil and created a series of canyons up to 150 feet deep. The Civilian Conservation Corps replanted trees in the 1930s in an effort to halt the erosion.*

palmetto tree was named a champion in the American Forests' National Register of Big Trees. Georgia's warm temperatures also encourage the growth of gardenias, wisteria, and a wide variety of other fragrant plants. The medicinal tonic ginseng grows wild in Georgia's Appalachian Mountains.

With the most coastline of any of the fifty United States except Alaska, Florida's sandy beaches are interspersed with both pine forests and mangrove swamps. The most remarkable feature of Florida, however, is the Everglades. This "river of grass," as some call it, is the largest swamp in the world, full of sawgrass, ferns, mangroves, mahogany, and slash pine. Fifteen native varieties of palm tree grow in the state, and hundreds more have been introduced.

Mistletoe, orchids, and poinsettias all can be found in the wilds of Florida.

Alabama is even more heavily forested than its neighboring states of Tennessee, Georgia, and Florida. The state has 125 varieties of trees, including pecan. It is particularly well known for its lushly flowering azaleas, dogwoods, rhododendrons, and mountain laurels. Eighty-acre Dismals Canyon in northwest Alabama features a natural arboretum of twenty-seven kinds of trees growing in close proximity. Next door to Alabama, Mississippi has some of the world's richest soil. Like Louisiana and Arkansas, it has large tracts of forest-covered wetland, although far less than was once the case. Named after the fine, yellowish soil, the Loess Hills are part of Mississippi's Gulf Coastal Plains, as

Below: This vintage barn can be found in northern Kentucky. Small farms continue to populate large sections of the state.

are the Pine Hills, which grow long-leaf and slash pine trees. Cottonwood, sweet gum, tupelo, and oak trees growing in Mississippi add to the broad range of plant life characteristic of that part of the South. These Southern marsh islands were left behind by the Mississippi River when it shifted course, discarding heaps of clay, sand, and debris. Farthest west of the South's states, Arkansas has pine, hickory, maple, oak, willow, and wild cherry trees. The South Arkansas Arboretum makes its home in El Dorado and is dedicated to preserving the state's native and rare plants.

A number of unusual or surprising wildlife species make their homes in the South. Virginia has more wild turkeys than Massachusetts, home of the pilgrims and Thanksgiving traditions. Its Shenandoah National Park has twelve varieties of salamander. White-tailed deer, black bears, foxes, raccoons, and opossums inhabit West Virginia. Kentucky adds to the list mink and woodchucks, as well as swamp rabbits, river otters, and cougars, although the latter are rapidly disappearing. Wild hogs live in Tennessee's mountains, and the state is known for its mockingbirds and bald eagles. North Carolina's black bears grow as large as 300 pounds in the Great Smoky Mountains, where there are also bobcats.

The sea islands off the coast of South Carolina have their own petite variety of deer, along with pelicans, ducks, and gulls. Some 400 varieties of fish are found along the state's coast, including dolphin, tuna, sea trout, and channel bass, and South Carolina's 400-pound loggerhead turtles lay up to 150 eggs in its beach sands. Many rare and endangered bird species visit Georgia's bird refuges. They include red-cockaded and ivory-billed woodpeckers, Kirtland's warblers, peregrine falcons, wood storks, and Bachman's warblers. Some of the 350 right whales left in the world swim in the waters off Georgia. Other rare wildlife types are the Florida panther, eastern cougar, humpback whale, gray bat, Indiana bat, West Indian manatee, and three kinds of turtles.

Above: *Mountain Laurel makes its home on the rock face of Little River Canyon in Alabama.*

Reptiles and birds top Florida's distinctive wildlife list. Once rare, alligators and crocodiles have thrived in cohabitation with the state's human population. The only habitat in the world where these two reptiles coexist is Florida's Everglades. An equally exotic Florida denizen is the manatee. Bird life is abundant and exotic, including spoonbills, egrets, ibis, flamingos, and herons. Florida's Keys have their own type of deer, the Key deer. The state's Merritt Island National Wildlife Refuge provides a home to 500 animal types in Florida. And more can be found in nearby Canaveral National Seashore.

Among the South's Gulf Coast states, Alabama has actively pursued wildlife conservation, for example, restoring habitat for ospreys, brown pelicans, great blue herons, bald eagles, and blue-birds. Mississippi is best known throughout the world for its catfish, although it has plenty of other game fish, like bream, crappie, and bass among freshwater species; and men-haden, speckled trout, and mackerel in the Gulf waters. Feral pigs with tusks run wild in Louisiana, which also provides winter quarters for many bird species, from the roseate spoonbill to some 15 million blackbirds. Perhaps the

Below: *This manatee is swimming underwater off Key Largo, Florida. The gentle, aquatic animals are a popular tourist attraction in many parts of Florida, but they are slowly disappearing because of injuries caused by motorboats.*

most unusual mammal of all to inhabit the South is the nine-banded armadillo, found in Arkansas and Florida.

To learn about the South's history is to learn how integral this region has been to the formation of America. After the settlement of Jamestown, farming for export quickly became highly profitable. The colonial Southerners did well and developed a lifestyle that both imitated and rivaled that of the mother country, England. The success of the early Southern plantation owners helps explain the South's resistance to changing its slave-dependent culture in the nineteenth century. This resistance led to what many would say was the nation's most devastating war. If the South did not want to give up its culture and lifestyle, even after it lost the Civil War, and held out against changing its attitudes towards African-Americans well into the twentieth century, it began to catch up later on. Today it has become one of the nation's most economically progressive regions.

Above: *These freshwater mullets were photographed underwater at Alexander Springs Recreation Area in Ocala National Park, Florida. The park permits snorkeling and scuba diving there to view the plentiful fish and underwater vegetation.*

Above: *Monticello, Thomas Jefferson's Virginia plantation, is a landmark of early American architecture. The young nation's third president, Jefferson worked on the property's design for forty years and described it as his "essay in architecture."*

Many Southerners have played distinguished roles in the nation's history. Virginia's colonists were integral to America's formation, from George Washington, who served his people as Commander-in-Chief of the Continental Army, to Thomas Jefferson, who wrote the historic Declaration of Independence. Both went on to serve as Presidents of the United States, Washington becoming the "Father" of the country after he was elected in 1789. Although General Robert Edward Lee led the Confederate Army to defeat at Appomattox in the Civil War, he is considered one of the nation's premier soldiers. Another of America's revered Presidents, Abraham Lincoln, was born in Kentucky. Other Southern Presidents include Kentuckian Zachary Taylor, Tennessean Andrew Johnson, and North Carolinians James Polk and Andrew Jackson (born in Waxhaw, on the border with South Carolina). One

of the nation's greatest Supreme Court Justices, Louis Brandeis, was born in Kentucky, as was Confederate President Jefferson Davis.

Alamo hero Davy Crockett was born in Tennessee, and when he represented his state in Congress, stood up for Native American land rights even though it got him defeated for his third term. In 1938 novelist Pearl Buck, born in West Virginia, received the internationally acclaimed Nobel Prize for Literature. Two of North Carolina's authors, William Porter, writing as O'Henry, and Thomas Wolfe, appear on most lists of noted American writers. Louisiana has produced writers Truman Capote and Lillian Hellman; and Mississippi boasts William Faulkner, Eudora Welty, Walker Percy, and Tennessee Williams.

Despite the South's history of segregation, many of its African-Americans have found a place in the nation's pantheon of the great. Louis Bruce, born a Virginia slave, later became the first African-American to serve in the U.S. Senate. Inventor George Washington Carver did most of his agricultural research at Tuskegee Institute in Tuskegee, Alabama, which was founded by Virginia-born civil rights activist, and writer Booker T. Washington. The father of the American Civil Rights Movement, Martin Luther King, Jr., was born in Georgia. Possibly the greatest blues singer ever born was Bessie Smith from Tennessee, and one of the world's greatest trumpet players, Dizzy Gillespie, hails from South Carolina. Another, Louis Armstrong, was born in New Orleans, Louisiana. The South has been the birthplace of many of the United States' native music forms, including jazz, blues, and bluegrass. It has also created some of the best regional American cuisine, from cajun-style catfish to ham hocks, collard greens, grits, and chitlins.

"The South always makes good reading," University of North Carolina Humanities professor and author Fred Hobson has written. "It features the virtues, writ large, of the nation as a whole. It's good entertainment. It's high drama." Rich in history, integral to the nation's founding, the South takes pride in its past and unique place in the nation. Northerner Walt Whitman has paid poetic tribute: "O magnet-South! O glistening perfumed South! My South! O quick mettle, rich blood, impulse, and love! Good and evil! O all dear to me!"

Overleaf: Boneyard Beach at Cape Romain National Wildlife Refuge, South Carolina.

Below: A view of the river front at Savannah, Georgia.

THE
FIRST
INHABITANTS

Previous page:
The Sipsey Wilderness of Alabama, located in the Bankhead National Forest, is known not only for its many natural attractions— waterfalls, rare birds, wildflowers—but also as one of the major sites in the Southeast of prehistoric Indian drawings and rock carvings.

The prehistory of the South—covering the many thousands of years before the first Europeans arrived—has much in common with the prehistory of other regions of the United States. But it also includes several most unusual developments and achievements that have left some distinctive imprints, both metaphorically on history and literally on the land. And when it comes to the series of great mounds that punctuate the land from the Atlantic to the Mississippi and from the Gulf of Mexico to the Appalachian range, the first peoples of the South produced a set of monuments that rank among the world's most admired.

The earliest humans to enter the South region were the same people who had been moving across the Americas since the first groups came over from Asia on the land bridge known as Beringia. (Some may also have made their way by boats.) Most authorities believe that these first groups entered North America about 15,000 BC, though that date is no longer universally accepted. Whenever the first humans entered North America, they were migrating through the Western Hemisphere surprisingly quickly, so that they were present in the South by about 12,000 BC. By 11,500 BC scattered bands seem to have penetrated all the way to the Atlantic coast, into the Appalachians, and down to the easternmost shores of the Gulf of Mexico.

These first Americans—now generally known as Paleo-Indians ("old" or "early" Indians")—were small groups of families constantly on the move in search of food. The women gathered nuts, berries, fruits, roots, and other edible vegetation, while the menfolk hunted the large game that still roamed the region—mastodon, bison, large bears, caribou. Their weapons and tools were made of stone—the former, varieties of the Clovis point found throughout most of North America during this era—so sources of usable stone would also have influenced their travels.

The environment they found in the South differed considerably from that of modern times. The last of the great Ice Ages was by then moving into its final phase, and although the great ice caps and glaciers had not reached down into the South, its climate was much cooler and wetter than today's. The vegetation in the mountains and foothills was like the tundra found in northern Canada today, while the species of trees were also those now associated with more northerly regions. Another major difference came about from the fact that the ice caps and glaciers had "locked up" so much of the earth's water that the world's sea level was lowered by as much as 150 feet. By the time humans would begin to settle along the coastal regions of the Atlantic and Gulf of Mexico, the sea levels were beginning to rise, but the coastal plain still extended much farther out. As a result, many of the earliest sites and remains of the Paleo-Indians in these areas have long been lost to the ocean water.

As these Paleo-Indians began to spread throughout the South, they also began to settle down. So long as they remained mobile, seasonal transients, they probably chose rock shelters and caves; thus remains of Paleo-Indians are found in Russell Cave in Bridgeport, Alabama, and the better known Mammoth Cave in Kentucky. Naturally, too, they recognized the need for good water supplies—and fishing soon supplemented their hunting—so that many of the Paleo-Indian sites of the South are found along rivers: the Big South Fork of the Cumberland River in Kentucky and Tennessee; the Chattahoochee River near Atlanta, Georgia; and the Ocmulgee River near Macon, Georgia. Other Paleo-Indian sites in the South include the John Pearce site in northwestern Louisiana, the Little Salt Spring and Warren Mineral Spring in Florida; the Jonesboro and St. Francis National Forest sites in Arkansas; and the Dalton, Suwannee, and Simpson sites located in Georgia.

By about 9000 BC, with the Ice Age now coming to a close, major environmental changes began to take place in the South. Average temperatures warmed up and the region became a temperate climate zone, with the flora and fauna much closer to those prevalent in modern times—deciduous forests, for instance, and smaller mammals such as white-tailed deer. (An exception, then as now, is the subtropical environment centered on the Everglades in Florida.)

The period that now ensued, known as the Archaic phase of culture of North American Indians, lasted until about 1000 BC, allowing for many variations throughout this vast region. Initially it is distinguished by the greater variety of material culture including carved stone bowls, baskets, nets, bone needles, even polished stone beads shaped like animals or insects. Their shelters, made of wood and vegetation, were now increasingly elaborate, and some Indians even began to make wooden canoes. Clothing was made from both animal hides and vegetation. Domesticated dogs were kept.

The use of wood and vegetation for so many of their artifacts means that few such objects have survived, but many stone tools have. These include axes, atlatls (spearthrowers), perforators, drills, choppers, specialized knives, and scrapers. One of the Early Archaic sites that has yielded the most is called Windover, near Titusville, Florida; in addition to all the usual stone tools, Windover has produced fish hooks, pins, shell adzes, wooden stakes and canoes, and even fragments of cloth and woven bags. Such finds support the view that the Archaic period witnessed the growth of more stable groups—settling down, that is, for longer periods and accumulating material possessions.

As the Archaic Period progressed, another development took place. In addition to the hunting, fishing, and food-gathering, these people began to extract large quantities of shellfish, both along seacoasts and rivers. This led to the establishment of "base camps" close to the waters, and in turn led to houses, prepared burials, and large storage pits. Along the southern Atlantic coast, people settled down to exploit the saltwater

Above: Since excavations began in 1951, the Russell Cave, in Bridgeport, Alabama, has yielded artifacts that attest to almost 9,000 years of continuous occupation by Native Americans.

Overleaf: The Apalachicola Forest, located in the Florida Panhandle along the border with Alabama, takes its name from a tribe of Native Americans encountered by the first Spanish to come into the area. Related to the historic Choctaw and Creek Indians, the Apalachicolas' own legends claim they came from the west— possibly Texas.

Right: *This is an artist's reconstruction of the Watson Brake Earthen Mound Complex in northern Louisiana. Dated to approximately 3400–1800 BC, it may be the oldest large-scale mound site in all the Americas. Although no specific artifacts have been found here, it is believed that the site may have had some ceremonial function.*

oyster beds. Along the Green River in Kentucky, people were augmenting a more varied diet with freshwater mussels. The burials at these Green River sites contain imported trade materials that testify to trade networks now expanding throughout the South and also suggest that a slightly more hierarchical society was developing—that is, some individuals were gaining more wealth and power than others, very likely from taking charge of the trading. Meanwhile, some Tennessee River burials suggest violent deaths that may have resulted from conflicts over control of local resources.

In Louisiana, too, by as early as 3400 BC, there are signs that people were beginning to build good-sized earthen mounds. Their exact function is still not known, for there have been no finds of human remains (indicative of burials) and no ceremonial objects (indicative of some religious function). The most

impressive of these sites is known as Watson Brake, near Monroe, in northern Louisiana; it may in fact be the oldest large-scale mound site in the Americas. Watson Brake consists of at least eleven mounds, ranging from 3 to 25 feet high and connected by ridges to form an oval some 850 feet across. It is believed that the people responsible for this structure were still mobile hunters-gatherers who may have come here only from summer through autumn to take advantage of the rich aquatic resources. There is no evidence of year-round occupation, and the material remains indicate they did not participate in any trading operations. The site was abandoned about 1800 BC, probably because the Arkansas River changed its course, making the area less attractive.

A related Late Archaic phenomenon—and equally mysterious with regard to the exact function—are the many large "shell rings" found along the Atlantic

Coast from the sea islands of South Carolina to northern Florida. These rings, which range from 130 feet to 820 feet in diameter and from 2 feet to 13 feet in height, were formed of discarded shells and other domestic materials.

Many people today find it hard to believe that such sophisticated structures would have been constructed unless they served some purpose—specifically, some sacred or secular ceremonial function. If this were the case, then these shell rings also suggest the existence of relatively settled and organized communities. One theory is that people made their homes in the cleared space at the center of the rings. Another is that the rings were built up when the Indians swept the central area of refuse to clear a space for special ceremonies. Still another is that, since these shell rings are located close to water, they may have somehow been used as fish traps. Contrariwise, other scholars point

to the fact that elsewhere throughout the South many Archaic Indians simply discarded shells and other refuse in what are known as "middens"—and these are just neat garbage dumps.

Unlike some of the Archaic earth mounds, the shell rings have not survived well. One that has been preserved is the Sewee Shell Ring in the Francis Marion National Forest, north of Charleston, South Carolina.

Most of the shell rings seem to have been made between about 2000 to 1000 BC. During that time, an even more impressive site was about to come into its own: the one named Poverty Point, near Epps, northeast of Watson Brake in northeastern Louisiana. Poverty Point consists of a complex set of earthen mounds and ridges: the central area consists of six rows of concentric ridges, originally five feet high; the diameter of the outermost ridges measures three-quarters of a mile. To the

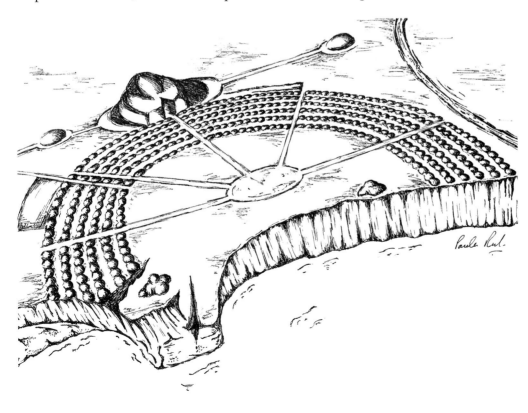

Left: Poverty Point, near Epps in northeastern Louisiana, is a complex of concentric earthen ridges and mounds; the most impressive of the latter is shaped like a large bird. It is attributed to the Archaic Indians and must have served as a ceremonial center.

west of the concentric ridges is the great bird-shaped Poverty Point Mound, some 700 feet by 640 feet at its base and 70 feet high. To the north is Mound B, 20 feet high and conical in shape.

Again, the exact function of Poverty Point is not known. Although some believe that the ridges were foundations for houses, there is almost no evidence of such structures. The conical Mound B was erected over ash and burnt bone fragments, and it is tempting to assume that Poverty Point was a site with some religious role; most archaeologists, however, are content to say it had some ceremonial function. One thing is clear: no one was buried in these earthworks.

Certainly Poverty Point was erected by a people who had a complex social organization and participated in extensive trading networks. The former is attested to by the sheer ambition of the site itself: anything on this scale could not be built without both organizers and laborers. (It has been estimated that it required some 5,000,000 hours to build these structures). The latter is attested to by the many tools, bowls, and other artifacts made from materials that had to be imported from distant locales including the Ohio River Valley and northern Georgia.

Poverty Point, which appears to have been abandoned about 700 BC, represents in many ways the peak of the Archaic period; the so-called Poverty Point culture both dominated the Late Archaic South and continued to exercise its influence for several centuries thereafter. But by this time, still more changes were occurring throughout the South, leading to a phase of culture among the many of the Indians who lived east of the Mississippi River; it is

Left: The white-tailed deer—here in St. Marks National Wildlife Refuge along the Gulf Coast of the Florida Panhandle—was one of the mainstays of the diet of Native Americans from about 9000 BC. It is still one of the most sought-after of game animals in parts of North America.

generally known as the Woodland Period and is considered to have lasted from about 1000 BC until AD 900. As always when history is divided into periods, this does not mean that the lifeways of the Indians of the South changed suddenly and dramatically. Indeed, two of the major "markers" of this Woodland period are now known to have actually got started by the end of the Archaic Period—that is, ceramic pottery and cultivated crops.

The earliest known ceramics in the United States have been found at a site on Stallings Island in the Savannah River, near Augusta, Georgia. The pottery that was made was fairly plain but some of it was decorated with incised or punctuated markings. This technology seems to have appeared in the South first along the south Atlantic coast, then spread westward to the coastal plains areas of Alabama and Mississippi, and soon was taken up throughout the South. Variations in production techniques, pot forms, and decorations also developed.

As for agriculture, it is generally believed to have been women who began to cultivate plants, as the men continued to hunt and fish. The women would have noticed both the best places to gather edible plants in the wild and also that these plants then reappeared each year where they had been disposed of near their settlements. Squash, gourds, and sunflowers were among the first plants cultivated in the South, as were plants now regarded as weeds but that have nutritious seeds, including maygrass, knotweed, and lamb's quarters. Only near the end of the Woodland Period does maize begin to appear as a cultivated crop in the South.

Both pottery and agriculture called for and supported more settled communities, and these also distinguish the Woodland Period. There was still some seasonal dispersal to search for food and other needed resources but by the late autumn and winter, people would gather together in relatively large settlements. More elaborate houses were built, as were cylindrical storage pits and earth ovens. Large trade networks developed, and goods from copper and other metals to conch shells began to appear throughout the South.

The population was increasing and, although the family remained the basic social unit, more sophisticated sociopolitical organizations were needed. Clearly, too, there were now emerging individuals who were richer, probably more important, and also likely more powerful. The evidence of this is in the series of burial complexes that appear in the South by about 200 BC—mounds in which exotic and ritual objects were placed alongside the bodies.

Not all mounds were for burials. At Ortona, Florida, just west of Lake Okeechobee, Indians who lived here about AD 250 had built elaborate sculptured earthworks, one of which resembled a crescent moon and star. They later built a 450-foot-long pond shaped like a ceremonial baton. They also built seven miles of canals, some 20 feet wide and 3 to 4 feet deep, which linked their settlement to the Caloosahatchee River and so to the Gulf of Mexico.

About AD 900, a new phase of culture had emerged in many parts of the South, one that has been given the name Mississippian. This name reflects the original notion that the culture's main features had first appeared in the

Mississippi River basin and were quite distinct from those of the Woodland Period. It is now known that many of these features began centuries before AD 900 and not necessarily in the Mississippi basin. But it was in the centuries following AD 900 that these cultural elements were widely adopted throughout the South.

Maize began to be adopted as the major crop; the cultivation of maize was accompanied by permanent settlements, now occuring increasingly along floodplains of large rivers. The rich soils were not only conducive to growing maize but also to squash and beans, and these three crops soon became the three staples of many of the Indians east of the Mississippi. Many of the traditional wild foods were still harvested—nuts and fruits—and men still hunted the smaller game such as deer, raccoon, turkey, but now they used the far more efficient bows and arrows. Food surpluses required storage facilities and supported a thriving trade for other resources. Pottery making advanced greatly, both in the technology that produced stronger vessels and in the shaping of more varied forms.

Below: *The Powhatan dominated much of Virginia when the first English arrived there in the late 1580s. Although this engraving depicts an elaborate dance ceremony from that era, it is virtually certain that these Indians had engaged in such a ritual for many centuries.*

Opposite: The Cohutta Wilderness of northern Georgia, here viewed from Fort Mountain State Park, was inhabited during the Mississippian culture phase by Indians sometimes known as Etowahian because the center of their society was the major town of Etowah.

Undeniably the most dramatic feature of the Mississippian Period, however, was the construction of the large mounds as the centerpiece of the larger towns. The towns were usually built around a central plaza that was used for major social and ceremonial occasions. On the edge of the plaza were one or more flat-topped mounds, which served as bases either for temples or for houses used by the priests and chieftains. Although the mounds have often been called "temple mounds," it is not clear

Right: This painting of a woman of an unknown Florida tribe was by the English settler/artist John White, but is probably based on the work of the French artist Jacques Le Moyne, who visited the French colony in Florida in the 1560s. She holds food containers—part of a culture that had changed little during the centuries before the coming of Europeans.

whether in some instances individual men held both offices. But it does appear that these men controlled the lives of the mass of the people, supervising religious and secular ceremonies that held their communities together, distributing the food necessary to sustain life throughout the years, organizing the trade that maintained their economic prosperity, and making new alliances or waging war with neighboring settlements. Many of these Mississippian towns were surrounded by wooden stockades or palisades, confirming the notion that armed conflicts were not unknown at this time.

The Mississippian mound sites located throughout the South are often grouped geographically. The Middle Mississippian area includes sites in western and central Kentucky, western Tennessee, northeastern Arkansas, and northern Alabama and Mississippi. The most ambitious of all the sites in this region was that at Moundville, south of Tuscaloosa, Alabama; this was both a popu-

lous town and a major ceremonial center, as attested to by the twenty-six mounds that surrounded the central plaza. The Lower Mississippi Valley, or Plaquemine Culture Area, includes the mounds in western Mississippi and eastern Louisiana, at sites such as those at Emerald, Winterville, Owl Creek, Jaketown, and Holly Bluff (Lake George) in Mississippi. The South Appalachian area includes sites at Etowah and Ocmulgee in Georgia, and at Shiloh National Military Park in Tennessee.

Although many Indians throughout the South continued to live much as they had been doing for many centuries, there is no question that the Mississippian Mound culture was the most dramatic and pervasive culture during the period that led up to the arrival of the first Europeans. Even when Indians in remote corners of the South did not erect mounds as ambitious as those in the Mississippian heartland, they often constructed burial and temple mounds. In Florida, for example, the Weeden

Right: These Choctaw warriors are depicted by an eighteenth-century French artist as displaying scalps. Probably descendants of the Mississippian Temple Mound builders, the Choctaw's first contacts with Europeans were with DeSoto and the Spanish, but from about 1700 to 1763, the Choctaw of Mississippi were important allies of the French.

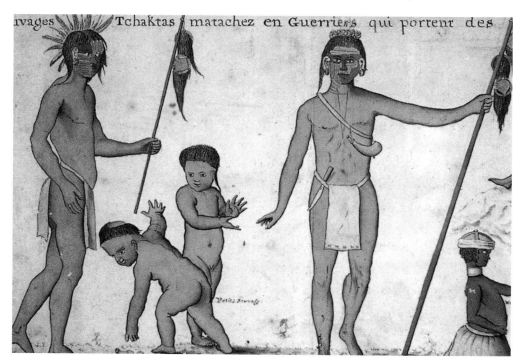

Left: This engraving by Theodor de Bry, published in the early 1600s, shows Florida Indians preserving animals by smoking them, as they had done for centuries before the coming of Europeans.

Island Culture, named from its "type site" in Tampa Bay, extended from southern Georgia and Alabama and down through northern Florida to Tampa Bay; its mounds are not especially impressive, but the Weeden Island people produced some of the finest and most delicately carved pottery made by Indians east of the Mississippi.

When the first Europeans appeared in the South in the mid-1500s, the Mississippian Mound culture was still thriving in some centers. There are numerous accounts both of the sites and of the activities, including ceremonies, at these locales, but in general the Mississippian Mound culture had begun to decline even before the coming of the white man. The reason for this decline remains as debatable as the explanation of the origins of the mounds. One view has been that the builders were directly influenced by the Maya and other mound-builders of Middle America; at the other extreme is the claim that the mounds were strictly indigenous—that their ancestry can be traced directly to the early mounds of the Late Archaic Indians.

Whatever the explanations for the emergence and decline of the mound-building cultures of the American South, they sustained a long-lasting and extensive range of complex communities. Some of the first Europeans who made contact would respect them, but all too many did not. Fortunately enough of the Indians' past has survived to allow modern people to appreciate this great chapter in America's history.

Overleaf: This empty conch shell lies along a beach of one of the Florida Keys. The conch was prized by Native Americans as a source of food, while its shell had several uses and was widely traded.

47

EXPLORERS
AND
EARLY SETTLERS

As early as the beginning of the sixteenth century, the American South was becoming a magnet for exploration and conquest by European nations jockeying to command the high seas and colonize North America. Most powerful among them was Spain.

Spanish nobleman Juan Ponce de León was one of the earliest explorers to reach the South. At the end of the fifteenth century, he traveled with Italian-born Christopher Columbus on his second voyage to the Americas. In 1508, Ponce de León sailed to Puerto Rico—then called Boriquen—discovered gold, and became the island's governor. In 1513 he set sail for the Bahamian island of Bimini, said by the native peoples to be the site of a wonderful fountain, but ended up landing at the future site of St. Augustine, Florida. Despite the popular legend, it is doubtful he was looking for the Fountain of Youth that still attracts tourists to St. Augustine today.

Right: The Italian-born explorer Christopher Columbus made four voyages to the New World on behalf of Spain's Ferdinand and Isabella, but landed only in the Bahamas and Caribbean region. It was Spaniard Juan Ponce de Leon, who traveled with Columbus on the second trip, who entered the history books as the first European to visit the American South.

Another early Spanish explorer, Pedro de Salaza, is credited with the second European landing in North America, in 1514 at Beaufort County, in South Carolina. He was followed in 1521 by Francisco de Gordillo. On the Gulf side of the South, Alonso Alvarez de Piñeda sailed into Mobile Bay in 1519, becoming the first European to visit what would later become Alabama.

Florida—*La Florida* in Spanish—acquired its name because Ponce de León arrived on Easter Sunday, or *Pascua de Flores*. He thought he had discovered an island and continued south from St. Augustine, exploring Florida's eastern coast as far as Key West, before traveling up the western coastline, and then turning back to Puerto Rico. Commissioned by the King of Spain to subdue the native people and establish a colony in Florida, Ponce de León returned in 1521. During a skirmish with Indians near Charlotte Harbor, however, the explorer suffered an arrow wound and died shortly after his return to Cuba. He never did start a Florida settlement.

Nevertheless, Spanish attempts to colonize Florida continued. Pánfilo de Narváez left Spain in 1527 after being named governor of Florida. He landed the next spring near Tampa Bay and searched unsuccessfully for gold near Tallahassee. Members of his party may have been the first to enter southern Alabama. Attacked by Native Americans and battered by storms, de Narváez and most of his men were lost along the Texas coast. In 1539 Spain's governor of Cuba, Hernando de Soto, landed in the Tampa Bay area and began another fruitless hunt for gold, silver, and gems. Before his death three years later, de Soto and his men traveled through much of the South: Georgia, North and South Carolina, Tennessee, Alabama, Mississippi, Louisiana, and Arkansas. De Soto's 1540 encounter in Alabama with the Choctaw, who were led by Chief Tuscaloosa or "Black Warrior," ranks as one of the worst of the early Spanish battles with Native Americans. In the battle of Mauvila, de Soto defeated the Choctaw, killing Tuscaloosa and many of his people.

In the sixteenth and seventeenth centuries, the Spanish regarded Florida as including all or parts of many other present-day Southern states. The first Spanish colony in Alabama, for instance, was started in 1559 near Mobile Bay by Tristan de Luna y Arellano. It was not successful, however. Farther north, the Italian explorer Giovanni da

Prom Lupi

Verrazzano, commissioned by King François I of France, touched shore at Cape Fear, North Carolina, and later at what was probably Kitty Hawk, on the Outer Banks of North Carolina, as early as 1524. He named the latter Arcadia because of its great beauty. Despite these explorations, however, St. Augustine, Florida, became the first permanent European settlement in America in 1565 and remains the nation's oldest city.

Florida could easily have been a French colony. In 1562, French explorer Jean Ribaut sailed up St. Johns River near present-day Jacksonville and claimed it for France. He continued his voyage, landing in South Carolina at what are now Port Royal and Parris Island. He established a colony he named Charlesfort, but this base was soon abandoned. A group of French Huguenots led by René de Goulaine de Laudonnière followed in 1565 and built Fort Caroline at the place where Ribaut landed. This spot is now marked by Fort Caroline National Memorial.

Above: *Ponce de Leon landed at what became St. Augustine, Florida, America's oldest city, and according to legend discovered the Fountain of Youth. The legend lacks authenticity, but today the city has an archaeological park where visitors can sample the spring water claimed to be Ponce de Leon's Fountain of Youth.*

Left: *An early map of Florida pictures French explorers sailing up the broad Port Royal River toward the area they named Lynx Point (Prom. Lupi in Latin) after they found Native Americans roasting a lynx cub there.*

Previous pages:
Alexander Springs Recreational Area in Ocala National Forest near Orlando, Florida, offers visitors many outdoor activities. Hernando De Soto and his men landed in Florida in 1539 on an entrada, *or exploration, and traveled through the area.*

Below*: An early image of fighting between Indians and Spanish forces illustrates the cruelty with which native peoples were treated by Europeans.*

In the meantime, Spanish naval officer Pedro Menéndez de Avilés was commissioned to establish the first Spanish colony in Florida and serve as its governor. First he had to dispose of the Huguenots at Fort Caroline. In 1565, when the French forces were debilitated by a storm, Menéndez de Avilés killed them and renamed their fort San Mateo. Florida was then firmly established as a Spanish colony, with settlements or watchtowers constructed at Cape Canaveral and Biscayne Bay. In 1566, Menéndez de Avilés added forts at St. Catherines Island, Georgia, followed by others on Cumberland, Sapelo and St. Simons Islands—all off the coast of Georgia. The Spanish named the region Guale District, after a friendly local tribe. The settlement at Santa Elena, which later became part of South Carolina, served as the capital of

Spanish Florida, which Menéndez de Avilés continued to govern until his death in 1574. Eventually this coastline would abound with both English and French pirates, the most famous of whom was Edward Teach, popularly known as Blackbeard, who was active here in the early 1700s. Legend has it that booty from Spanish galleons that were raided by Teach is still buried on Blackbeard Island in Georgia.

After the Spanish had sacked Fort Caroline, France did not try to colonize larger Florida again until the late seventeenth century, when French explorers traveled to the western Gulf coast. In an attempt to keep them away, the Spanish built a fort near Pensacola. Although the French made exploratory excursions in other parts of the South like western Georgia, their prime target was the Mississippi River Valley.

Spanish explorer de Soto had arrived at Sunflower Landing, near Helena, Arkansas, in 1541, but it was the French who built the first settlement in that state. In 1673 Louis Jolliet and Father Jacques Marquette traveled by canoe down the Mississippi as far as the Arkansas River, and as early as 1669, René-Robert Cavalier, best known by his title Sieur de La Salle, canoed down the Ohio River past Kentucky. In 1682 he claimed the entire Mississippi Valley for France, including parts or all of fifteen states, those in the South being Kentucky, Arkansas, Louisiana, and Mississippi. He named this vast region Louisiana after Louis XIV. One of his officers, Henri de Tonti, built a trading center, known as the Arkansas Post, in 1686 at a Quapaw village near the fork of the Arkansas and White Rivers. As Arkansas's first European settlement, it is marked by a National Memorial and Museum at Gillette. Two Frenchmen, Pierre Le Moyne, Sieur d'Iberville, and his brother Jean-Baptiste, Sieur de Bienville, landed near Ocean Springs, Mississippi, in 1698 and established a settlement that served as the capital for France's Louisiana Territory.

England was another serious rival to Spain during early colonizations of the South. In 1586 Sir Francis Drake landed at St. Augustine, Florida, and sacked it. He also raided missions built by the Spanish along the Georgia coast. His strategy of hit-and-run attacks against competing colonies continued until the English succeeded in establishing their own settlement farther north at Jamestown, Virginia, in 1607.

Perhaps because of America's close ties with England, Jamestown is commonly thought of as the nation's earliest

European settlement, when in fact it is merely the earliest permanent English settlement. St. Augustine predated Jamestown by more than forty years, and other Spanish settlements existed in the sixteenth century. A ship sent by Lucas Vásquez de Ayllón arrived in Winyah Bay, South Carolina, in 1521. Having enticed nearly 150 local Indians to come aboard, the Spanish sailed back to their colony, Santo Domingo, with the Native Americans as prisoners. Vásquez de Ayllón insisted that they be returned, but one named Chicora stayed behind, regaling Vásquez de Ayllón with tales of his wonderful home (which was also known as Chicora). Taking 500 Spaniards with him, Vásquez de Ayllón sailed to Winyah Bay to see for himself. He established a Spanish colony called San Miguel de Gualdape in South Carolina as early as 1526, but most of the colonists starved or died of disease, and the rest abandoned it.

Above: *The remains of Fort Raleigh on Roanoke Island, now a National Historic Site, located north of Manteo, North Carolina. The site memorializes Sir Walter Raleigh's colonies and the birthplace of Virginia Dare, the first English child born in America.*

Jesuit missionaries from Spain, led by Juan Baptista de Seguera, settled near Jamestown in 1571 but were killed the following year by the Powhatan. The English first arrived in North Carolina in 1585 on Roanoke Island on a scouting expedition financed by Sir Walter Raleigh. In 1587 the first settlers, financed again by Raleigh, arrived on Roanoke Island with John White as governor. His granddaughter Virginia Dare became the first child of American colonists born there. White left the fledgling colony to get supplies from England, but his return was delayed by the war between England and Spain. When he finally landed in 1590, the Roanoke Island settlement was empty with no sign of what had happened except for the word *croatoan* carved on a tree. It was the name of an apparently friendly local Indian tribe, and there is speculation that it may have indicated where the

settlers went. According to colonial historian Mary Beth Norton, they may actually have survived until 1606, since Native Americans told White about "blonde-haired" people who had only recently been killed in internecine warfare.

England's Jamestown colonists were organized by the London Company, which, like the Plymouth Company, had been granted a charter to colonize America's East Coast. They named their settlement Virginia after Elizabeth I, the virgin queen. Captain John Smith led the Jamestown colony. The settlers chose a somewhat soggy spit of land on the James River that has since become an island. In the first year alone, two-thirds of the settlers perished, and Jamestown came close to being abandoned in 1609–10 after a particularly harsh winter in which the region experienced its worst drought in history. Then Baron Thomas de la Ware, appointed as the new colony's first governor, arrived and brought in fresh supplies.

The purpose of the Jamestown colony was to turn a profit for the London Company's investors. A secondary goal was conversion of the native peoples to Christianity. In land area, the colony included parts of many of the lower 48 states; it also reached northward into Canada and as far east as the island of Bermuda. Most critically, it infringed on the lands of the native Powhatan Confederacy. As a result, the colonists found themselves attacked repeatedly by the Powhatan. Legend has it that the colonists' leader, Captain John Smith, was captured in a raid and released with help from Pocahontas, daughter of the Powhatan leader (who was eponymously named Powhatan). In fact, it was not so, although Smith himself cir-

Right: Pocahontas, who was christened Rebecca upon her conversion to Christianity, is portrayed here as a princess. Born around 1595 to Algonquin chief Powhatan, she first saw Europeans in 1607. As the bride of John Rolfe, she was later presented at court to King James I and members of England's aristocracy.

culated the story. Pocahontas meant "playful one" in the native dialect. Pocahontas's real name was Matoaka, and she was christened Rebecca after her conversion to Christianity. In 1613 she was kidnapped by the English, who hoped to use her to bargain with the Powhatan for the colony's well-being. She didn't marry Smith, but another colonist, named John Rolfe, by whom she bore a son before she died in 1618 in England, having been presented at court as an Indian princess.

If Pocahontas's rescue of John Smith is the stuff of legend, the importance of her people to the colony's survival is not. The Powhatan taught the English colonists how to raise such native crops as squash, corn, and beans, to hunt deer and turkey, and catch fish with weirs.

Pocahontas's husband Rolfe crossed the local tobacco strain with tobacco seeds from Trinidad and sent the dried leaves to Europe. Four barrels were sent abroad

in 1614, and by 1628, the annual export had grown to 500,000 pounds. Known as the "chopping Herbe of Hell," tobacco was grown by the colonists in such quantities that the soil was quickly exhausted.

As their farms grew too large to be run alone, the colonists imported indentured servants who worked off their debts or punishments for petty crimes in return for their labor. Most of them came from England and Ireland until 1619, when the first Africans arrived on a Dutch Indies ship and were traded for food. These African-Americans were listed as servants in Jamestown's records of 1623–4, and it is unclear whether they were slaves or indentured servants. The first African-American specifically named as a slave appears in Jamestown's court records in 1640. The number of African-Americans in Virginia totaled 300 in 1650. New York—the colony of New Netherland—actually had more slaves than the South as late as 1670.

Above: Tobacco quickly became a major cash crop in the American South of the seventeenth century, even though it was already considered the "chopping Herbe of Hell."

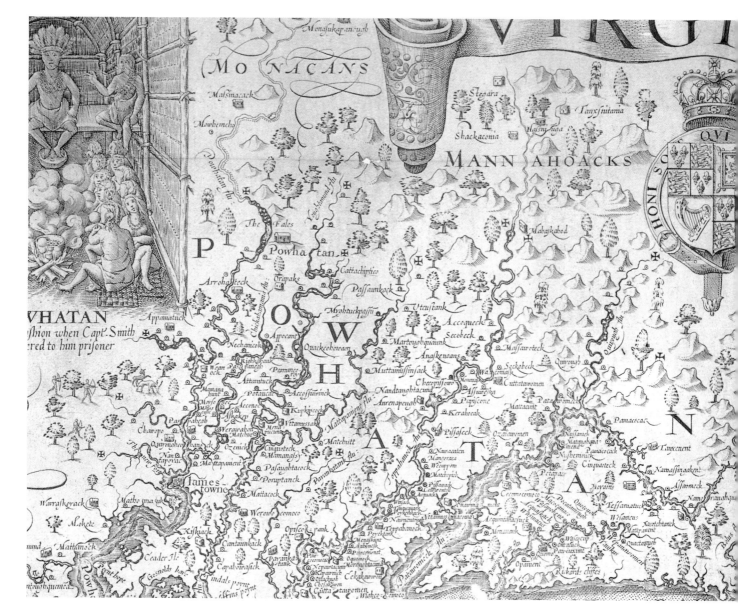

Above: *Captain John Smith headed the seventeenth-century Virginia colony funded by Sir Walter Raleigh. His map of the colony, first published in 1612, lists such Native American tribes as the Algonquian Powhatan and their enemies, the Sioux-speaking Manahoack and Monacan.*

Although a few wives had accompanied settlers in 1611, English women did not arrive by shipload at Jamestown until 1619. Like African-American slaves later, they were treated as a form of chattel. The first ninety who docked in Jamestown married the settlers who had paid their passage, at a cost equivalent to the price of 120 pounds of tobacco. Also in 1619, the colony's first elections were held, forming the New World's first representative government. It was called the House of Burgesses and shared power with a Virginia Company governance body.

Loath to let tobacco's riches line only private pockets, King James I established Virginia as a royal colony in 1624, rescinding the Virginia Company's charter. Due to the wealth accrued from tobacco, class divisions formed very early in Virginia. The earliest settlers, with land in the Tidewater region, became wealthy within little more than a generation. Those with land in the interior "frontier" did not have as easy a time. When England instituted trade laws that lowered the profit level of tobacco, they suffered more than the Tidewater colonists of bigger farms. In

Plantation. King Charles II made a gift of the Southern Plantation first to Robert Heath, then to eight royal supporters in 1663. The name Carolina came from the Latin meaning "land of Charles." Originally named by the Huguenot settlers of the "Lost Colony" for their King Charles IX, it served for the English King Charles II just as well. By 1670, the first settlers came from Barbados with their slaves and began building a new settlement they called Charles Towne at Albemarle Point on the Ashley River. William Drummond served as governor for Albemarle, the name given to the northern section of what was one large colony of Carolina. Ten years later, Charles Towne—today's Charleston—was moved to Oyster Point to take advantage of a better harbor. One of the colonists, Dr. Henry Woodward, lived with the Cusabo for four years, learning their language and developing lucrative trade connections.

In Virginia, tensions grew until Nathaniel Bacon organized the western colonists in 1676 to revolt against Governor William Berkeley. An English aristocrat himself, Bacon was related to the philosopher Sir Francis Bacon as well as to Berkeley's wife. When Berkeley did not marshal forces against the Native Americans who were attacking farmers in the interior, Bacon made two successful forays against the Indians, not always distinguishing between which groups were friendly and which hostile. Then he attended the House of Burgesses as the representative for Henrico County and demanded that Berkeley commission further raids. Power seesawed back and forth between Bacon and Berkeley, until Bacon burned Jamestown. The rebellion ended after

Overleaf: Sapelo Island, Georgia's fourth largest barrier island, was first settled by Spaniard Lucas Vasquez de Ayllon who brought 500 men, women, and African slaves. Franciscan priests built missions, followed by Jesuits, who named the island Zapelo after a Jesuit priest. A Jesuit convent, the Mission of San Jose de Zapala, lasted on the island from 1573 to the end of the 1680s.

addition, the local Native Americans were resentful of relinquishing ever more territory and more readily attacked colonists away from the relatively well-populated Tidewater region. Royally appointed governors often operated as absentee administrators and were unresponsive to the needs of the interior, favoring instead the new Tidewater aristocracy.

By the 1650s, English colonists were moving into what became North and South Carolina. To distinguish themselves from the settlements farther north, they called theirs the Southern

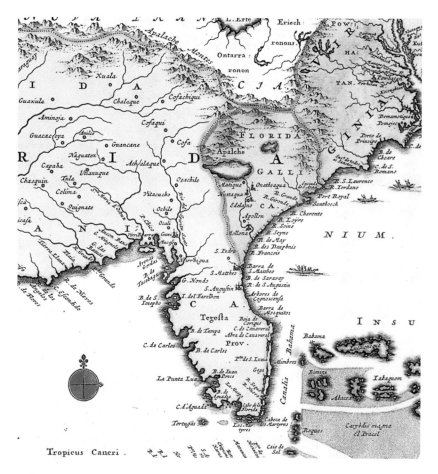

Above: Dutch mapmaker Nicolaes Visscher charted Florida in a map published around 1690. In the seventeenth century, the colony was still divided into Spanish (Hispanica) and French (Gallica) sections.

Bacon died of the "Bloodie Flux," most likely dysentery. The Tidewater colonists continued to dominate the settlement, and reforms did not come to pass. Because he had sided with Bacon, Albemarle's Governor Drummond was put to death. In the aftermath of Bacon's Rebellion, a North Carolina colonist named John Culpeper seized power there and led that section of Carolina for two years.

West Virginia would not exist as a separate state until the Civil War. When Virginia seceded in 1861, its forty western counties formed their own government and achieved statehood as West Virginia in 1863. Some two centuries earlier, a German-born mapmaker, John Lederer, traveled through the area three times for Governor Berkeley in 1669 and 1670, reaching the Blue Ridge Mountains

and viewing the Shenandoah River Valley. The next year, Thomas Batts and Robert Fallam explored as far as New River, which to their surprise flowed west rather than toward the Atlantic. Their travels into Kentucky and the surrounding region enabled the British to claim the Ohio River Valley. While crossing the Appalachian range, they found a series of tree carvings with the letters MANI, now thought to be initials of Europeans who arrived before them. In 1673, fur trader James Needham traveled into the Appalachians in an effort to establish trade with the Yuchi. With him was sixteen-year-old Gabriel Arthur, who stayed behind with the Yuchi and is believed to be the first European to visit West Virginia's Kanawha Valley and northeastern Kentucky.

The story of early explorations and settlements in America's South would not be complete without further mention of the Native Americans encountered there by early Europeans. In Florida, Mission San Luis de Apalachee near Tallahassee represented the westernmost center of the Spanish mission settlements and was named for the Apalachee who inhabited the area. Florida's early Spanish missions among the Timucua people were destroyed by the English and their Native American allies. Southwestern Florida's Calusa were known as the Shell People. In Alabama and Georgia, Europeans encountered the Tuskegee, as well as the Okmulgee and Yemasee peoples of the Creek Confederacy. The Catawba, or River People, of South Carolina, once 10,000 strong, were quickly decimated by European diseases like smallpox. A similar fate awaited the Tutelo and Tuscarora in North Carolina.

De Soto was the first to make contact with Mississippi's Choctaw in 1540. He also encountered the Cherokee of Tennessee and described their large, agriculturally based villages in his writings. Jacques Marquette encountered the Arkansas, or Quapaw, people during his explorations of the Mississippi River. Kentucky, which during the early colonial days of the American South was part of Virginia, probably acquired its name as an Iroquois variation on the name of the local Shawnee village in Clark County, Eskippathiki, which means "salt licks." Natchitoches, in Louisiana, founded in 1714 and the oldest permanent settlement in the state, was named after the Natchitoches people who traded with the French there.

By about 1700, the Native Americans and settlers in the South had attained a certain equilibrium. Although there had been many skirmishes between the early explorers and those whose lands they were intruding on, and even a few more serious conflicts—in particular, between the Powhatan and the Virginia colonists in 1622 and 1644—in general, the colonists and the native peoples of the South were living in a manner that has been characterized as "wary cooperation." As the settlers increased in number and spread out, this relationship would inevitably change.

Overleaf: The Everglades stretch out near Whitewater Bay in south Florida. Hernando de Soto and his soldiers were the first Europeans to travel through the Everglades.

Below: Nineteenth-century painter William Powell depicts the "Discovery of the Mississippi by Hernando de Soto, AD 1541."

FORGING
THEIR
DESTINIES

Previous page:
Fort Frederica was established to protect Georgia from Spanish attacks three years after the colony was founded. Located on St. Simons Island, the fort was at the time the southernmost British garrison in North America.

If Spain dominated early exploration and settlement of America's South, Britain's sphere of influence grew as the British colonies developed in Virginia and the Carolinas. Spain and France continued to exert control in Florida and Louisiana—Spain's Franciscan missions in Florida were particularly important—until the end of the century. For the colonists who ultimately declared independence in 1776, however, the issue was English control.

Economics influenced Britain's push for colonization, since the commercial opportunities the colonies offered fed global trade, the seedbed for capitalism. Virginia survived in the earliest days and thrived in the eighteenth century because of tobacco, a crop that offered an export value ten times greater than any other at the time. It also exhausted the soil, usually within three years, but seemingly endless sources of new land lay to the west. Today we think of the frontier as west of the Mississippi River. In fact, it lay much farther to the east in the eighteenth century, just beyond the Virginia and Carolina tidewaters in the Piedmont region—the foothills of the Appalachians.

The most economically and politically advanced section of the South in the eighteenth century consisted of greater Virginia, which still included West Virginia, and greater Carolina. Greater Virginia was dominated by 350 colonist families. Once the Navigation Acts—a series of laws that were passed by Parliament to control trade, starting in 1651—lowered profits on tobacco, these planters maintained their affluent status by planting more or becoming land speculators, selling land to German and French Huguenot and Scots-Irish immigrants. Anglican com-

missary Reverend James Blair pushed for Virginia's first educational institution, and the College of William and Mary received a royal charter in 1693.

In many ways, these founding families tried to fashion themselves after the English aristocracy. They sent their children to English schools and built large, English-style "manors." Stratford Hall Plantation provides a good example of the "trophy houses" characteristic of affluent eighteenth-century Virginia. It was constructed in 1738 by Thomas Lee, a founder of the Ohio Company, acting Governor of Virginia, and the father of Richard Henry Lee and Francis Lightfoot Lee, both signers of the Declaration of Independence. (Robert E. Lee was born in Stratford Hall.) With twin wings, the central portion of the brick house, built in the popular Georgian style, has a massive stairway leading to a central doorway on the second level of the building.

As more and more new settlers moved in, they expanded Virginia west toward Pennsylvania and the Ohio River. By 1722 the Virginia government encouraged such expansion by providing government-owned land rent-free for ten years. This move displeased the French, who claimed all lands north of the Ohio River and were themselves expanding into western Virginia. A Welsh settler, Morgan Morgan, moved to western Virginia from Delaware in 1726 and founded at Bunker Hill what is believed to be the first settlement in the section of Virginia that later became West Virginia. German immigrants established New Mecklenburg, now called Shepherdstown, in 1727. The town may date back to 1719, when it was called Potomoke, and the first church in what

is now West Virginia was founded there by Presbyterians. In 1734 Robert Harper began his ferry business a little farther south at the confluence of the Potomac and Shenandoah Rivers—the site of Harpers Ferry of Civil War fame. In Boone County, West Virginia, in 1742, John Peter Salley discovered coal. This find eventually led to one of the state's most important industries.

After Carolina was taken over by the eight friends of King Charles II—called lords proprietor—it was divided into three districts: Albemarle, Clarendon, and Craven. Resentful of long-distance governance by the lords proprietor, Albemarle's colonists rejected one English governor after another, until 1691, when England sent one for the entire colony of Carolina. By the last decade of the seventeenth century, settlers began calling Albemarle "North Carolina," and in 1729 Carolina was finally divided into North and South Carolina, each with its own governor.

Built on the Pamlico River at the site of an Indian village, Bath is North Carolina's oldest town, and the state's first library opened there in 1700. New Bern is a port city started in 1710 by English explorer John Lawson and Baron Christopher de Graffenreid, leader of approximately 2,000 German and Swiss immigrants. As the North Carolina colonists developed their economy, they began taking hunting

Above: This highly romanticized 1872 Currier and Ives print, "The Old Plantation," portrays carefree African-Americans dancing in front of slave quarters near the plantation where they most likely worked.

lands from a local Iroquois tribe, the Tuscarora, without permission or compensation. Slave traders also abducted Tuscarora women and children, selling them to other colonies as slaves. Slavers themselves, the Tuscarora appealed to the colonists unsuccessfully to stop the trafficking. They captured Lawson, by then the colony's surveyor general, then tried and executed him. Fighting under Chief Hencock, the Tuscarora also killed 130 colonists. South Carolina came to its neighbor's aid with a force of colonists and Indians led by Colonel John Barnwell. Strife continued off and on until March 1713, when hundreds of Indians were killed. The Tuscarora never recovered. The survivors migrated to New York, eventually forming the sixth nation of the Iroquois Confederacy.

In addition to Native American raids, another hazard endured by North Carolina's early settlers was assault by pirates, who lurked in North Carolina's coastal inlets. Edward Teach, also known as Blackbeard, was finally killed in 1718 after a clash near Okracoke Island. The lords proprietor sold their languishing colony to King George II in 1729, and once it became a royal colony, newcom-

ers flooded into the area. By 1775 North Carolina's non-native population had leapt to 350,000 from 35,000 in 1730.

The establishment of Georgia, last of the original thirteen colonies, began in 1733 at what is now Savannah under the supervision of British Colonel James Oglethorpe. The new colony provided a haven for England's poor, many of whom were in debtors' prison, and for Europeans suffering religious persecution. Georgia served to increase trade between England and the colonies and, importantly, it also acted as a political cushion between South Carolina and Florida, which remained in unfriendly Spanish hands.

France, and to a lesser degree Spain, continued to challenge England's domination of the South's colonies until the French and Indian Wars—actually four separate wars lasting from 1689 to 1763—resolved the matter. Hostilities didn't reach the South until what is known as Queen Anne's War began in May 1702. Because Spain allied itself with France, Carolina sent a force of 500 settlers and Native Americans to St. Augustine, Florida, razing most of the town. The war continued in New England, and fighting did not return to the South until 1704. Then Governor James Moore led Carolina colonists and Native Americans in a foray against Spanish settlements located in southern Carolina and Georgia. Since Spain's claims to Carolina dated back to the seventeenth century, when it built most of its missions, Moore's victory was an important one. In retaliation, French and Spanish soldiers attacked Charles Town in August 1706 but were rebuffed. Although England and France signed the Treaty of Utrecht in 1713, ending the

Left: The Chapel of Ease on St. Helena Island in South Carolina is in ruins after a forest fire destroyed it in 1886. It was built in 1742 and used for worship by planters who lived on the island.

JOIN, or DIE.

Right: The rattlesnake was a favorite symbol for colonists before the Revolution. The Gadsden flag, with its epithet "Don't Tread on Me," was presented to South Carolina's congress in 1776 by Christopher Gadsden, after whom it was named. Gadsden, a delegate to the Second Continental Congress, intended the flag to be used by America's naval commander-in-chief.

In 1754, Benjamin Franklin published an image of a snake cut into eight sections (far right), each representing one of the original colonies, including Virginia, North Carolina, and South Carolina from the South. The segmented snake symbolized the danger of disunity. Still a royal province, Georgia was not included.

Queen Anne War, it took many more years before the South's colonies became decisively English.

The period of 1713–39 remained relatively quiet. Nevertheless, South Carolina colonists found themselves under attack by the Yamasee, Creek, Choctaw, and Catawba in 1715. The colonists fought back the next year, and with help from the Cherokee defeated the Yamasee near Port Royal, South Carolina. Yamasee at Nombre de Dios, a Spanish mission at St. Augustine, were attacked by South Carolinians in 1728.

Following an incident in 1731 when Spanish soldiers boarded an English merchant ship in the West Indies and cut off the captain's ear, England declared war on Spain when the preserved ear was presented before a committee of the House of Commons in 1738. The War of Jenkins' Ear lasted from 1739 to 1741. Georgia's Governor Oglethorpe captured two Spanish forts in Florida during 1740, although he did not succeed in taking St. Augustine. Spanish retaliation began in 1742 at the Battle of Bloody Marsh when their troops landed on St. Simons Island, but Governor Oglethorpe fended off the attack with brilliant tactics and kept the southern border of the colonies intact.

The final conflict, which gave its name to this extended series of disputes among the European nations over their colonies—the French and Indian War—began in 1754. It was preceded by one of the first military assignments for a youthful George Washington. Virginia Governor Robert Dinwiddie sent the twenty-one-year-old major to reconnoiter new French forts along the Ohio River. Later that year, Washington headed a Virginia militia detachment sent to protect a fort on the Ohio River near the northernmost junction of West Virginia and Pennsylvania. When the militia engaged French soldiers, the French and Indian War of 1754–63 began. Most of the war was fought in Pennsylvania and farther north, but at the urging of Washington the colonists built forts along the Potomac River in Virginia as well as in South Carolina. As a result of the war, France ceded its Louisiana territory—including the South's Arkansas and Louisiana—to Spain in an effort to keep it out of English hands. The 1763 Treaty of Paris turned all French territory east of the Mississippi River, except New Orleans, over to England. Spain gave Florida to England in exchange for Cuba.

From its inception in 1732 until 1752, the new colony of Georgia was administered by a group of crown-appointed trustees. Initially they did not allow settlers to rent or sell their land holdings, which were limited to 500 acres each. Only men could inherit land, and it was illegal to import slaves from Africa, and liquor. Few settlers found the trustee's oversight to their liking, but once royal governors began administering the colony in 1755, the situation changed. An elected assembly and a plantation system were established, and new crops such as indigo and rice were introduced.

After the Treaty of Paris was signed, westward expansion of the colony, which had been confined to the coastal area by unfriendly Spaniards and Native Americans, became possible.

The South's Gulf states—Alabama, Louisiana, Mississippi, and Florida—had a different history than its Atlantic colonies during the eighteenth century. After Tristan de Luna's brief Spanish

Below: *A detail from John Mitchell's 1755 map shows the colonies of North Carolina, Georgia, and Florida. The map was used to set the nation's boundaries under the 1782–3 Treaty of Paris that ended the Revolutionary War.*

Below: Conecuh National Forest is located in southern Alabama, just above the Florida Panhandle. The territory of Conecuh, a Muskogean Indian word for "land of cane," remained in dispute by the Spanish, British, and Americans until the 1795 Treaty of Ildefonso assigned it to the United States.

settlement at Mobile, Alabama, was abandoned in 1561, Europeans did not settle there again for nearly 150 years. The French brothers d'Iberville and d'Bienville built a fort on the Mobile River in 1702. Fort Louis became the first permanent European settlement in what would be Alabama and served as the capital of Louisiana colony. Once New Orleans became Louisiana's capital in 1720, Fort Louis was renamed Fort Condé. It underwent a second name change after the French and Indian War, when England dubbed it Fort Charlotte. The Louisiana colony itself changed hands a dizzying number of times.

Louisiana began as a French royal colony. In 1712, France assigned exclusive trading rights in the region to a French merchant, Antoine Crozat. When the arrangement failed to prove profitable for him, Crozat turned it over to a company run by a Scot, John Law, who in turn deceived investors in what became known as the "Mississippi Bubble." In 1731, Louisiana resumed its status as a royal colony, but when it still showed no profit, France gave the Isle of Orleans and the Louisiana section of the colony to Spain. Ocean Springs, home of d'Iberville, became the first capital of the Louisiana colony, while

Left: Castillo de San Marcos overlooks Matanza Bay in St. Augustine, Florida. It was built as a fort by the Spanish between 1672 and 1695 and remained continuously under Spanish control until 1821, except for a brief British period (1763–84) after the French and Indian War.

d'Iberville's brother d'Bienville founded New Orleans in 1718. After the French and Indian War of 1754–63, many French Acadians from Nova Scotia, forced out by the English, migrated to Louisiana. Cajuns, the name used to describe many Louisianians today, is a variation in pronunciation of Acadians.

After La Salle claimed the entire Mississippi Valley for France in 1682, French settlers began moving into Mississippi. One of the first was Louis Juchereau de St. Denis, who was based at Fort St. John in Louisiana in 1701. He was later in charge of Fort Biloxi. To keep the rival English traders at bay, d'Iberville built Fort Maurepas east of Biloxi in 1699. Fort Rosalie at Natchez followed in 1716. By 1731 the French colonists had decimated the resident Natchez. In the South's other Gulf coast colony, Florida, most of the resident Native Americans had died by the beginning of the eighteenth century, probably from diseases carried by the Spanish. Starting in 1702 and 1704 with Carolina, English colonists and their Native American allies invaded Florida

to destroy the Spanish missions and enslaved the rest of the native peoples. Native Americans from Alabama and Georgia moved in to fill the breach, sometimes at Spain's invitation, and formed the Seminole tribe. Once England acquired Florida from the Spanish in exchange for Cuba at the end of the French and Indian War, they divided it into West and East Florida, with capitals in Pensacola and St. Augustine. East Florida was the more successful, but, like Georgia, both relied on heavy subsidies from England.

During the eighteenth century, the South's interior, consisting of the future states of Kentucky, Tennessee, and Arkansas, remained the least developed. Arkansas Post, Arkansas, which was originally French, became Spanish in 1673. The settlement remained an important center of trade, particularly with the Quapaw, who provided protection for the settlers. Arkansas Post also served as a strategic supply point during the Revolutionary War.

In Tennessee in 1714, Frenchman Charles Charleville established a fort near what became Nashville. The resident Cherokee and Chickasaw fought on the English side during the French and Indian War, while the Creek fought with the French. During most of the eighteenth century, Tennessee was still part of North Carolina. Cut off from that colony's government by the mountains, Tennessee's settlers formed the Watauga Association in 1772. It was the first time an American colony tried to start an independent and democratic government of its own.

Several explorers passed through neighboring Kentucky in the seventeenth century, and in 1750 Dr. Thomas Walker discovered the Cumberland Gap while looking for land as an agent of the Loyal and Ohio development companies. Daniel Boone entered Kentucky through the Cumberland Gap during his first trip there in 1767. He returned in 1773 with a group of settlers, but they were soon ousted by the local Native Americans. A year later, these same native peoples sold their rights to all land south of the Ohio River—what is

now Kentucky. James Harrod also started Kentucky's first permanent European settlement, Harrod's Town, in 1774, and Daniel Boone built Fort Boonesborough on the Kentucky River in 1775. Once Kentucky became part of Virginia in 1776, more and more settlers arrived from neighboring colonies like Pennsylvania and Maryland, as well as Virginia. Like their neighbors in Tennessee, however, they were cut off from the rest of the main colony by the terrain and suffered attacks from Native Americans armed with British weapons.

The English government believed the colonists should help pay for the French and Indian War. Parliament passed an import tax, the Sugar Act, in 1764, followed the next year by the Stamp Act. Virginian Patrick Henry spoke out vehemently against the Stamp Act, saying "if this be treason, make the most of it." Many colonies began boycotting British products. Responding to the pressure, Parliament repealed the odious Stamp Act in 1765 but replaced it with the Declaratory Act, proclaiming England's right to tax the colonies. Soon, Committees of Correspondence, intended to keep colonists abreast of the growing discontent, cropped up in many colonies, including Virginia in 1774. A British tax on tea caused the next uproar in all the colonies. As a result, tea sat untouched in a warehouse for three years in Charles Town. After Parliament passed the Intolerable Acts of 1774—a series of punitive measures directed at the colonies—the first Continental Congress met in Philadelphia. Of the Southern colonies, Georgia was the only one not to send a representative, but it did promise to support any decisions that were made.

Right: Daniel Boone is the best known of the settlers who traveled though Kentucky during the eighteenth century. He became legendary for his exploration, land development, and taming of the wilderness.

At the start of the Revolutionary War, race became an issue in the South. In 1775 England's governor of Virginia, Lord Dunmore, encouraged African-American slaves belonging to "rebels" to abandon the colony's plantations and join the British army. Virginian Thomas Jefferson drafted the Declaration of Independence, and it was officially approved by the Second Continental Congress on July 4, 1776.

In the early stages of the Revolution, most combat went on in the North. By April 29, 1779, after the patriot general William Moultrie retreated to Charles Town, South Carolina, following an engagement with British troops across the Savannah River, Georgia was occupied by the British and acquired a royal governor. The British Navy attacked Portsmouth and Norfolk, Virginia, on May 10. General Casimir Pulaski, a Polish-born noble who had joined the Continental Army, saved Charles Town from British attack on May 11. Then the French sailed to Savannah Bay to join forces with patriot general Benjamin Lincoln and help wrest Savannah, Georgia, from British hands.

The single largest American loss of the war occurred in South Carolina on May 19, 1780. After more than a month of fighting, General Benjamin Lincoln formally surrendered Charles Town to England's General Clinton, who was convinced the South would join forces with England as a result. But it never happened. Once Charles Town was lost, the Continental Congress appointed Horatio Gates to lead American forces in the South. They had dwindled to between two and three thousand and all but disappeared after a major defeat on August 16, 1780, at Camden, South

Left: *General Casimir Pulaski, known as the "father of the American cavalry," is honored in many parts of America for his role in the 1779 Battle of Savannah.*

Below: *A satirical 1775 engraving by Philip Dawes, "A Society of Patriotic Ladies." It depicts colonial women in Edenton, South Carolina, organizing to boycott tea imported from England.*

Carolina. Nearly 1,000 were killed or wounded, and General Gates himself retreated on horseback. Following his defeat of American forces at Camden, British General Cornwallis marched into North Carolina. In a turning point for American fortunes, Virginian Colonel William Campbell led 1,000 men into the Battle of Kings Mountain and defeated the British, firing at them with frontiersmen's accuracy.

In 1781, turncoat Benedict Arnold led 1,200 British troops in an attack on Richmond, Virginia. Perhaps the most ingenious American maneuver of the Revolution took place on January 17, 1781, in Cowpens, South Carolina. Colonel Daniel Morgan routed British Colonel Banastre Tarleton by arranging his forces in three lines. Once the first, less experienced line shot two rounds, they moved back and let the next line attack. Tarleton mistook the line rota-

Below: This 1846 Currier and Ives lithograph depicts Cornwallis as handing over his sword to George Washington after surrendering at Yorktown. In fact, Cornwallis did not attend the ceremony, sending instead his second-in-command, so Washington arranged for the sword to be handed to one of his own subordinates.

tion for retreat. The American cavalry encircled the British forces, and the patriots quickly defeated them. After an inconclusive battle at Guilford Court House, Cornwallis withdrew to the coast of North Carolina. Instead of pursuing him, Greene went south toward Lord Francis Rawdon's troops in South Carolina. He did not defeat the English at Hobkirk's Hill, but he inflicted damaging casualties. Spain had also taken up arms against the British, and by May

of 1781, Spanish Governor Bernardo de Gálvez captured Pensacola, Florida, and took control of the western part of Florida from the British.

Meanwhile, Cornwallis moved into Virginia, planning to join forces with Arnold and take over that colony. Colonel Tarleton, who was traveling with him, took his cavalry forces to Charlottesville, Virginia, hoping to capture Virginia Governor Thomas Jefferson by surprise. He missed the American patriot by minutes. In August, British forces under Cornwallis dug in at Yorktown on the coast of Virginia and waited for reinforcements. In effect, the British general had been pushed north, and British troops in South Carolina were losing ground. French ships arrived at Chesapeake Bay in August, and Washington, after marching his troops down to the bay from New York, was in position outside Yorktown by late September.

Above: Francis Marion National Forest in South Carolina is named for the Revolutionary War hero. Nicknamed the "Swamp Fox," Marion harassed British troops in guerilla warfare and eluded capture by disappearing into the swamps.

Above: This period painting depicts the ladies and gentlemen who gathered in Fredericksburg, Virginia, to celebrate the British surrender at Yorktown with a peace ball.

British reinforcements, sent by General Henry Clinton from the West Indies, arrived, but the French flotilla attacked their ships, preventing them from reaching Cornwallis in time. Led by Washington, the Marquis de Lafayette, and the Comte de Rochambeau, the combined French and American forces of 18,000 encircled Cornwallis and his 7,000 men. The battle was over; Cornwallis surrendered on October 19, 1781.

In what is considered the final Revolutionary engagement, Colonel George Rogers Clark led a cavalry force of over 1,000 from Kentucky into Ohio country on November 10, 1782. They punished the Shawnee for their attack with British troops on American forces at Licking River near Lexington, Kentucky, almost two months earlier.

The first articles of peace between Britain and the new United States of America were signed on November 30, 1782. The new nation stretched from Maine to Georgia. (The status of Florida remained to be settled between Britain and Spain.) The northern border was set at the forty-fifth parallel, and the Mississippi River created the western boundary. September 3, 1783, marks the date of the final Treaty of Paris. It was eventually ratified by the Continental Congress on January 14, 1784.

During the aftermath of America's war of liberation, Virginia continued to spearhead the formation of a new government. Virginian James Madison led the effort to write a constitution, and George Mason was responsible for the Bill of Rights. Virginia became the tenth state when it ratified the Constitution in 1788. It also provided the new nation with four of its first five presidents: George Washington, Thomas Jefferson,

James Madison, and James Monroe. A number of the South's current states, once subsumed by larger colonies, came into existence. Kentuckians held a convention in Danville and achieved statehood in 1792, with Frankfort as their capital. In 1795, Spain ceded most of Alabama back to the U.S. Tennessee began to take shape after settlers in the western section of North Carolina signed the Cumberland Compact in 1780. They established their own state in 1784, and called it Franklin after Benjamin Franklin. Franklin lasted until 1788, when it rejoined North Carolina after failing to win congressional recognition. Temporarily called the Territory of the United States South of the River Ohio, Franklin was part of what would become the sixteenth state, Tennessee, in 1796. Mississippi Territory was created by the federal government in 1798 and consisted of what is now eastern Mississippi and Alabama. Still held by Spain, Florida was the only section of the Southeast that did not belong to the new United States.

As the eighteenth century came to an end, the Southern states busied themselves with government-building and economic development. Northerner Eli Whitney, while visiting a plantation outside Savannah, Georgia, played an important role in 1793 by devising an invention to speed up the processing of cotton. His cotton gin revolutionized the cotton business and helped make "King Cotton" the most important component of the South's economy. Big changes were afoot for the South at the beginning of the new century, when the huge Louisiana Territory changed hands twice, ending up as part of America.

Overleaf: Cotton ripens in a Southern field. The South Carolina Cotton Museum in Bishopville has exhibits and an interpretive history of what proved the lynchpin of the nineteenth-century Southern economy.

Below: Workers processing cotton on an early version of the cotton gin, invented by Eli Whitney. By greatly increasing production, the machine fueled the demand for more slaves.

STRUGGLING
FOR
UNITY

Previous page: Fallen Confederate soldiers are memorialized in Georgia with this gravestone. An estimated 260,000 Confederate soldiers died in the Civil War.

Like much of the rest of the fledgling United States, the South was still taking shape at the opening of the nineteenth century. Two main events—the Louisiana Purchase and the "War Between the States"—dominated the region's history during that century.

Most state boundaries in the South remained fluid well into the nineteenth century. During the years of the Revolution, many of the original thirteen colonies still held large claims to unsettled lands in the West. Soon the well-established former colonies of Virginia, Georgia, and North and South Carolina were joined by new, inland states like Kentucky and Tennessee. West Virginia, however, would not separate from Virginia until the Civil War. Although England yielded western Florida to Spain in 1781, along with Pensacola and eastern Florida two years later, American settlers from the other Southern states quickly began moving in. Isolated from the rest of Spain's colonial holdings, Florida would become an American territory in 1821.

Through the secret treaty of San Idelfonso in 1800, Spain restored the giant Louisiana Territory to France. Once President Thomas Jefferson learned France had the Louisiana Territory, he instructed Thomas Livingston, the Paris-based American diplomat, to purchase what he called "the isle of Orleans" (New Orleans and West Florida) from France. With France facing the prospect of war with Britain, the timing was right, and the United States succeeded in buying the Louisiana Territory for $15 million. The momentous purchase agreement, which included the settlement of claims by American citizens against France, was signed on October 21, 1803.

The Louisiana Purchase expanded the size of the United States by 140 percent, adding territory that would become thirteen states or parts of states at a cost of roughly three cents an acre. Besides opening up new land for farming and boosting the fur trade, the Louisiana Purchase established the right of the federal government to buy land and ended the presence of other nations along the western frontier. The year after the Lousiana Purchase was completed, Congress divided it into two territories: Louisiana and Orleans. Orleans Territory, the region south of the 33rd parallel, became Louisiana, the nation's eighteenth state, in 1812, with New Orleans as its capital. The rest remained known as Louisiana Territory. Neighboring Mississippi Territory, created out of British West Florida after the Revolution, was eventually divided into two future states: Mississippi joined the Union in 1817 as the twentieth state, with Natchez, a major port, as its capital; and Alabama joined as the twenty-second state in 1819.

America's disputes with the former European colonial powers did not end with the American Revolution. One contentious issue that contributed to the War of 1812 was the British impressment of American sailors. Some 2,500 of them were treated like deserters from the British navy, even though they were American citizens. This, and other long-standing disputes came to a head in 1812, and the United States declared war on Great Britain. Meanwhile, frictions were developing between the Creek peoples and the United States over President George Washington's policies of assimilation, which put pressure on Native Americans to shed their ways in favor of Anglo-American culture. With a full-scale war underway, the British exploited Native American discontent by encouraging attacks against Americans.

Fighting came to the South on July 27, 1813, in the Battle of Burnt Corn Creek, when Creek forces attacked and overcame American militiamen north of Pensacola, Florida. They struck a second time at Fort Mims, north of Mobile, Alabama, and killed some 400 Americans. U.S. retaliation came in the Battle of Talladega in Alabama, where General Andrew Jackson's men killed almost 300 Creek. Then, on November 29, 1813, General John Floyd's soldiers killed a further 200 Creek in their village at Auttose, Alabama.

The decisive battle in this phase of the War of 1812 was fought at Horseshoe Bend on the Tallapoosa River in northern Alabama on March 27, 1814. Jackson led militia from Kentucky and Tennessee against Creek forces there and killed 700. At the end of the battle, Creek Chief Red Eagle looked for Jackson's tent and surrendered to him. The Treaty of Fort Jackson was signed on August 9, 1814. It required the Creek, many of whom were not involved in the anti-American activities, to surrender some 20 million acres of their land.

The British tried to take New Orleans, starting with an unsuccessful attempt by their navy to capture the port at Mobile, Alabama. Although the signing of the Treaty of Ghent officially ended the war on Christmas Eve, 1814, British General Edward Pakenham was not aware of this treaty and engaged Jackson's forces, who were dug in at Rodriguez Canal outside New Orleans. On January 8, 1815, the Battle of New Orleans began—and ended just a half-hour later. General Pakenham was killed, and the British took heavy losses. It was the last land battle of the War of 1812.

The Creek Confederacy, along with most other tribes east of the Mississippi River, lost millions of acres of land and never again took up arms against the Americans. But one Creek tribe, the Florida-based Seminole, resisted the consequences of American control. Settling in Florida during the eighteenth century, the Seminole gave haven over the years to many escaped slaves, most of whom became free, since Florida was controlled by Spain until 1819. Florida was also home to African-American slaves of the Seminole. The presence of African-Americans in Florida helped motivate the American government to keep the state from becoming a refuge for escaped slaves or falling under Native American control.

Below: Lithographer James Baillie's portrait of General Andrew Jackson shows him on horseback as the "Hero of New Orleans." Lasting only half an hour, the Battle of New Orleans was the War of 1812's last land battle.

The three Seminole Wars were waged periodically from 1817 to 1858. These wars were fought in Florida and nearby parts of Georgia. The first ended quickly when General Andrew Jackson invaded Pensacola and Fort Barrancas in May 1818. The second war dragged on for more than seven years, when the Seminole resisted evacuation to Indian Territory in Oklahoma and Arkansas after passage of the Indian Removal Act of 1830. Led by Chief Osceola, the Seminole waged guerrilla warfare against the U.S. military, who greatly outnumbered them. In 1837 Osceola was duped into a truce meeting and arrested. He died in prison in 1838. The war ended in 1842 when the few remaining Seminole agreed to stay west of Lake Okeechobee.

The final Seminole War was fought from December 1855 to March 1858. By then, only 500 Seminole remained in Florida. White settlers wanted them gone, however, and frictions between the two led to recurrent attacks. No treaty marked the end of these tragic wars. The last group of 163 Seminole, including 41 prisoners of war, sailed to New Orleans and continued on to Indian Territory. The remaining few who stayed behind in Florida were confined to reservations in the Everglades and Big Cypress Swamp.

The Cherokee of western Georgia chose a different route. By the time the Indian Removal Act of 1830 was passed, the Cherokee had become as assimilated as any Indians in the United States. At first they tried to resist removal to west of the Mississippi by using the U.S. court system, but in 1835 a group of Cherokee signed a treaty agreeing to

Below: *"Attack of the Seminoles on the Block House" portrays an incident during the Seminole Wars, most probably at Fort King near the Withlacoochee River.*

removal. In 1838 U.S. army troops under General Winfield Scott rounded up thousands of Cherokee men, women, and children and started them on a forced march of 1,000 miles to Indian Territory in Oklahoma. Before their "removal" was completed, some 4,000 Cherokee died on what would become known as "The Trail of Tears."

A few years of relative peace and prosperity throughout the South followed the Seminole Wars before the War Between the States—as the Civil War was called in the South—broke out in April 1861. Tensions were on their way to the boiling point well before that. In October 1859, at Harpers Ferry, Virginia (West Virginia had not yet been estab-

Above: *Harpers Ferry, West Virginia, the site of John Brown's famous 1859 attack on the U.S. arsenal, is located at the confluence of the Shenandoah and Potomac Rivers.*

Left: *Robert Lindneux's famous painting of Cherokee traveling on the Trail of Tears.*

Above: In his famous mural at the Topeka, Kansas, state capitol, Kansas native John Steuart Curry depicts the abolitionist John Brown as a wild-eyed fanatic. After Brown tried to raid the Harpers Ferry arsenal on October 16, 1859, to initiate a slave revolt, he was caught, tried, and executed.

lished), abolitionist John Brown tried to raid the federal arsenal to supply guns for a slave uprising. Brown and his followers were captured, tried for treason, and hanged.

Two related, unresolved issues faced the United States after independence and led to the outbreak of the Civil War. First was the question of whether an individual state could withdraw from the Union. Second came the matter of slavery, and since the South's economy depended heavily on slavery, it was at loggerheads with the North over the latter's call for abolition.

In 1860, America had in aggregate four million slaves, owned, surprisingly, by only 25 percent of Southerners. The numbers varied from state to state, with Mississippi on the high end at 50 percent and Maryland on the low end with 12.5 percent. While the North and

Midwest were developing industrial economies by the mid-nineteenth century, the South invested in slave labor and maintained a traditional agrarian economy, growing cotton, sugar, and rice. In March 1861, newly inaugurated U.S. President Abraham Lincoln promulgated the illegality of secession and slavery, although he also said the federal government would not intervene in cases where slavery already existed.

South Carolina led the way in withdrawing from the Union in December 1860. The federal government responded by beefing up its garrison at Fort Sumter in Charleston, South Carolina's harbor. Six more Southern states—Mississippi, Florida, Alabama, Georgia, Louisiana, and Texas—followed South Carolina out of the Union. North Carolina, Virginia, and Arkansas would join them the next year. Tennessee was the last of the states to secede, due to the pro-Union position of then-senator Andrew Johnson. The renegade states met in Montgomery, Alabama, and organized a provisional government. It emphasized states' rights but otherwise followed the U.S. Constitution. Kentucky-born Jefferson Davis was made president of the new Confederate States of America.

Before the actual outbreak of war, Southerners began seizing federal forts. A Confederate detachment rowed out to Fort Sumter and demanded that the garrison commander Major Robert Anderson surrender. Waiting for the arrival of reinforcements, Anderson temporized. Confederate General Pierre Beauregard ordered the fort fired upon. The first missile was launched early on the morning of April 12, 1861. Despite heavy Confederate fire, Fort Sumter's walls were not breached. Buildings within the garrison caught fire, though, and Anderson surrendered on April 13. Two Union soldiers died in the attack, and the rest set sail for New York.

No formal declaration of war was made by Congress, which did not want to give European nations an excuse to recognize the Confederacy. When Lincoln called for volunteers to put down this "insurrection," Kentucky, North Carolina, and Tennessee refused to commit any soldiers. Meanwhile, Richmond, Virginia, became the new Confederacy's capital city, and the Confederacy officially declared war. Virginian Robert E. Lee, considered the nation's foremost military leader, was offered command of the Union army. He declined, however, saying, "I cannot raise my hand against my birthplace, my home, my children," and resigned from the Union forces.

At the start of the war, the South, with a preponderance of the nation's best soldiers, had a military advantage. The North, however, had greater numbers, more wealth, and greater industrial resources. More than 200,000 African-Americans, mostly freed slaves, served with the North's forces in one capacity or another. The largest number, 24,000, came from Louisiana. The Confederacy was reluctant to use African-Americans, almost all of whom were slaves, and didn't enlist them until 1865, close to the end of the war.

Below: In this photograph from Mathew Brady's documentation of the Civil War, an African-American Union soldier oversees a cooking fire and pots. Although Brady did not take all the pictures attributed to him, he is often regarded as the father of photojournalism.

Previous pages: Fort Clinch on Amelia Island in Florida was built starting in 1847. Confederate troops occupied it at the beginning of the Civil War; federal forces retook the fort in 1862. The site became a state park in 1935, with improvements made by the Civilian Conservation Corps.

Below: This vintage picture portrays the Confederate battery on the move during the first Battle of Bull Run (July 21, 1861) at Manassas, Virginia, near Washington, DC. The Confederates were victorious and forced the Union Army to retreat.

Since the North was attempting to subdue the secessionists, the South had the defensive advantage. If they held firm, they could in effect win the war. Their less-developed railroad system, however, created a disadvantage. The North's greater industrialization meant the Union could build warships and other necessary material.

Early combat was crucial in Virginia and the Southern border states of Maryland and Kentucky. Kentucky declared its neutrality on May 16, 1861, and would become the only Southern state not to join the Confederacy. By July, Manassas, Virginia, a railroad center strategically close to Washington, DC, became the site of fierce contention. The Confederates forced a Union retreat and, elated, claimed victory. The first of two battles for Manassas—known to Northerners as the Battles of Bull Run after the small Virginia stream where they were fought—memorialized the Confederate's "Rebel Yell" and earned Confederate General Thomas Jackson his nickname "Stonewall."

In the Western Theater, fighting proceeded in what became West Virginia and continued in Kentucky, which found itself "carved up" by competing Union and Confederate troops. Recognizing that slaves could be used against the North even if they didn't serve in the Confederate Army, Congress passed the Confiscation Act on August 6, 1862, which freed any slaves used by the Confederacy in non-military capacities when captured by Union forces.

Naval history was made in early March of 1862, when the first encounter between two ironclad boats—the Confederate *Virginia* (formerly the USS *Merrimack*, which had been captured and fully refurbished) and the USS *Monitor*—resulted in a draw. Several months later, the *Virginia*'s crew blew up their craft, rather than allow it to fall into Union General George B. McClellan's hands. In New Orleans, on May 1, Flag Officer David Farragut took possession of the city, and closed the mouth of the Mississippi River to Confederate traffic.

The second year of the war also brought important battles in Mississippi and Virginia. In Shiloh, Mississippi, Confederate General Beauregard went to sleep on April 6, thinking he had defeated General Ulysses S. Grant. The courage of the Union soldiers the next day gave the Union victory instead. Confederate General Lee initially prevailed, but Union forces made gains in Tennessee (more battles were fought there than any other state save Virginia) and in Kentucky. In a crucial battle at Fair Oaks (also known as Seven Pines) from May 31 to June 1, 1862, Confederate forces under General Joseph Eggleston Johnston stopped a Union advance on the South's capital, Richmond. It was followed at the end of the month by another series of engagements, called the Battles of the Seven Days. Lee kept the Union Army of the Potomac from advancing on Richmond.

The second Manassas/Bull Run campaign began on August 29, 1862. Lee, with assistance from General James Longstreet, turned back Union forces but missed the chance to wipe out Lincoln's Army of Virginia. In early September, Lee crossed the Potomac River and headed for Washington, DC. His battle plans fell into Northern hands, revealing his strategy to McClellan. Casualties were high for both sides at the Battle of Antietam in Maryland on September 17. By the end of the day, it was a draw, although the Union claimed victory. A total of 5,000 men died and 18,000 were wounded—the largest toll of the war—and it was the turning point for the North. Less than a week later, President Lincoln issued the Preliminary Emancipation Proclamation, refocusing the spotlight on the call to end slavery.

With a new commander of the troops, General Ambrose Burnside, the Union aimed its sights on Fredericksburg, Virginia. The carnage was great, with Union General Winfield Hancock losing almost half his troops. Meanwhile, Grant moved into Tennessee and Kentucky by boat, capturing Forts Henry and Donelson. As a

Below: The historic battle between the CSS Virginia (the former USS Merrimack) *and the USS* Monitor *took place on March 8–9, 1862, at Hampton Roads off the coast of Virginia. It was the first naval battle between two ironclad vessels.*

Above: *This view of Richmond, Virginia, on April 2, 1865, shows the Confederate capital in flames. Fires were set by the retreating Confederate loyalists who tried to destroy anything that could be of value to the advancing Union forces.*

result, the Confederate forces had to abandon Nashville, Tennessee. This was the first Confederate state capital to fall. Other battles, at Corinth, Mississippi; Perryville, Kentucky; and Pea Ridge, Arkansas, added to the North's momentum. Grant's campaign against the Confederate fort at Vicksburg, Mississippi, began as 1862 drew to a close.

One of the most important battles of the War Between the States took place in 1863. Along with Port Hudson, Louisiana, Vicksburg, Mississippi, was a strategic fort for the South. It guarded the Mississippi River, the main supply route for the South. The Siege of Vicksburg lasted from May 23 to July 4. The Union troops outnumbered the Confederates three to one, and by the end of the siege, Confederate soldiers had run out of food. Southern General John Pemberton surrendered to Grant after forty-eight days. Chattanooga, Tennessee, was the site of another important Union victory, led by Sherman and Grant. In June, the North

accepted West Virginia's petition to join the Union as the thirty-fifth state.

By 1864 the South was on its way to defeat, but the year unwound with heavy fighting and loss of life for both sides. In the Red River Campaign, during the first half of 1864, General Nathaniel Banks led the assault on Confederate strongholds in Louisiana and Alabama. Arkansas, now in the Union camp, abolished slavery on March 18, and New Orleans followed suit on April 6, as the 13th amendment abolishing slavery went through the Constitutional process. Confederate desertions increased.

The Union strategy for capturing the South's capital at Richmond started with an assault on Petersburg, where four railroad lines met. In June the Confederates staved off Union forces. By the next month, Northern soldiers had built a 500-foot-long tunnel, and they blew up the South's earthwork defenses at Petersburg. The ingenious ploy failed, since Confederate troops quickly closed the breach.

General Sherman began his famous march to Atlanta on May 7, 1864. Union troops occupied Atlanta beginning on September 4, and Sherman evacuated the city's residents. The details of Atlanta's burning have been vividly described in Margaret Mitchell's novel, *Gone With the Wind*. From Atlanta, Sherman started across Georgia to the port of Savannah on December 12, 1864. Before Sherman could attack, though, Confederate forces abandoned the city.

President Lincoln had been re-elected president in November 1864, and Tennessean Andrew Johnson was now his vice-president—an attempt to win over moderate Southerners. When 1865 arrived, Sherman was ready to storm North and South Carolina. At the end of March, Grant took aim at Lee's army in the Appomattox Campaign, and the Confederacy came to an end in all but name. Lee's retreat was cut off at Appomattox on April 9. He declared, "Then there is nothing left for me to do but go and see General Grant, and I would rather die a thousand deaths." Appearing in full dress uniform, he surrendered formally to Grant at the home of Wilmer McLean.

Although no festivities attended the surrender at Appomattox Court House, the end of the war was celebrated in Washington, DC, with a 500-gun salute. Less than one week later, President Lincoln was assassinated by actor John Wilkes Booth while attending a play at Ford's Theatre. He died on the morning of April 15, 1865. All fighting in the tragic War Between the States ceased on May 26, 1865, when New Orleans Confederates surrendered.

Below: Confederate General Lee's April 9, 1865, surrender to Union General Grant at the home of Wilmer McLean in Appomattox Courthouse, Virginia, is depicted here. Grant had written to Lee: "The result of the last week must convince you of the hopelessness of further resistance on the part of the Army of Northern Virginia in this struggle."

Above: This engraving by Thomas Nast for an 1867 edition of Harper's Weekly *comments on the impact of Lincoln's 1863 Emancipation Proclamation. One image pictures a man being sold as punishment for a crime, and the other shows the symbolic figure of justice turning a blind eye to a cruel beating.*

Under the terms of Lee's surrender, Confederate soldiers were paroled, allowed to go home, and assured that they would not be tried for treason if they adhered to Union laws. North Carolina lost the largest number of soldiers—one quarter of those fighting for the Confederacy—of any Southern state. Florida became the only Southern state whose capital, Tallahassee, was not captured by Northern troops.

In the summer of 1865, the South lay in ruins, its railroads wrecked, its major cities razed, its fields stripped bare. Yet four million African-American slaves tasted freedom for the first time. The islands of Manhattan and Martha's Vineyard might make noises about independence a century later, but no

longer did the notion of secession have any credence in the United States of America. Three post-Civil War amendments to the Constitution ensured the abolition of slavery (13th), provided a federal guarantee for individual rights (14th) and gave every male citizen the right to vote (15th). These civil commitments, however, took many years to fulfill in the South.

The first post war priority was the political status of the Confederate states. Lincoln's 1863 proclamation of pardon for any Confederate who swore to uphold the Union and its Constitution established the necessary precedent for rejoining the Union. The procedure was tried in Virginia, Louisiana, Arkansas, and Tennessee during the war. Lincoln's legislative opponents, however, passed the Wade-Davis bill, limiting new state governments to bona fide Unionists. Lincoln never signed the bill, but proposed letting states choose either course of action, and they chose the more lenient one. Andrew Johnson, Lincoln's successor after his assassination, followed Lincoln's amnesty plan in general, although he excluded property owners of $20,000 or more. It was an attempt to shift political power out of the hands of wealthy plantation and slave owners. The Freedman's Bureau was set up on March 3, 1865, to protect black interests. By the end of 1865, only Texas had not returned to civil government.

Although the South's economy was in shambles, many Northerners could think only in terms of punitive measures. Nor did the South willingly give African-Americans the vote, as the North wanted them to. On April 9, 1866, a Civil Rights Act was passed over President Johnson's veto. It extended the life of the Freedman's Bureau and provided protection from the Black Codes—Southern state legislation that controlled almost all aspects of the lives of freed slaves. The Reconstruction Act was passed the same year, dividing the South into five military districts (except for Tennessee), and in effect establishing military control over the defeated states.

The agents of the Freedman's Bureau and other organizations set up by the Reconstruction Act became known as carpetbaggers and scalawags. "Carpetbagger" came from the bags in which Northerners carried their belongings and "scalawag" was a Southern term used to describe useless cattle. Most were opportunists, but by controlling the black vote, they dominated state politics. When doubts were raised about the constitutionality of the 1866 Civil Rights Act, it was reformulated into the 14th amendment. By 1868, Florida, Alabama, Louisiana, and South Carolina ratified the 14th amendment and were readmitted to the Union.

The Republican Party, controlled by carpetbaggers, scalawags, and newly elected African-Americans, helped bring progressive reforms to the South, although it also gained a reputation for corruption. Standing behind them, over President Johnson's resistance, was Congress, which passed "force laws," to make Southern states comply with federal reconstruction legislation. The first force law was employed against South Carolina, when it passed a states' rights nullification ordinance.

Below: This Thomas Nast illustration critiques the actions of the South's anti-freedman organizations, the Ku Klux Klan and the White League, suggesting that African-American families were worse off after the Civil War, despite the end of slavery.

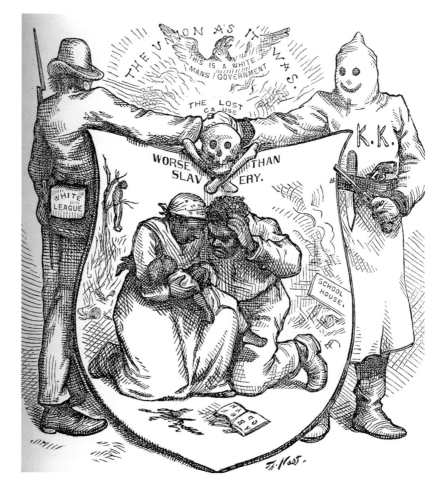

Below: In this photograph from the Mathew Brady collection, African-Americans line up before a school at a freedman's village in Arlington, Virginia. Such villages were set up by the North during the Civil War for freed slaves.

After fulfilling the requirements of the 15th amendment, Mississippi, Georgia, Virginia, and Texas were readmitted to the Union in 1870. Mississippian Hiram R. Revels became the first African-American elected to the U.S. Senate.

The profound political and social change the South underwent during Reconstruction inspired the growth of right-wing, racist organizations like the Ku Klux Klan, which began in Tennessee as a secret veterans club in 1866. It rapidly evolved into a terrorist organization, promoting beatings and murders of African-Americans and their supporters. Lawlessness ruled in many states, where Klan nightriders terrorized non-supporters. By 1876, most of the South's states had freed themselves from Republican control. By the end of the nineteenth century, African-Americans of the South were not much better off than before the War Between the States. They were subject to poll taxes, literacy tests and many other Jim Crow laws designed to keep them from voting, let alone holding political office or serving on juries. (Jim Crow was a derogatory term for early Black reformers).

On the South's horizon, however, was the industrial revolution. It would eventually bring not only new prosperity but a greater acceptance of the nation's broader social values.

The South at Work

Previous page: Florida oranges, today a major part of the state's economy, were first cultivated in 1579. In 1892, the USDA established the first federal laboratory in the state to support the citrus industry. By 1948, the USDA and the Florida Citrus Commission had developed frozen orange-juice concentrate.

Perhaps no region in the United States experienced more dramatic changes during the nineteenth century than the South, when it came to developing new occupations. In large part this was due to the fact that the South industrialized later than the rest of the nation and did not readily relinquish its agrarian, slave-based economy. Throughout most of the nineteenth century, it remained primarily agricultural. An interesting, little-known fact is that manufacturing was forbidden before the American Revolution in some Southern colonies, in order to keep them dependent on imported English products. "King Cotton" ruled, both on plantations where slaves did the work and on small independent farms. Once Eli Whitney's cotton gin made processing this fibrous plant easier by separating the lint from the seed, cotton became the South's major cash crop. In 1800, American farmers—with the South in the lead—produced 73,145 bales, each weighing 400 pounds. That figure jumped to 2.1 million bales by 1850.

The growing of cotton in both Virginia and the Carolinas dates back to the early eighteenth century. Two varieties—long-staple, Sea Island or black seed; and short-staple, highland green seed—predominated. Because the cultivation of cotton did not require elaborate planting, harvesting, or storage techniques, or equipment, cotton farming spread quickly. A Mexican variety, Petit Gulf, was imported to Mississippi in 1806 and increased the yield significantly.

Once the War of 1812 was over, British demand for American cotton meant new plantations developed in the South. More slaves were imported—from other states, since importing them from abroad was

Right: Magnolia Plantation in Natchitoches Parish, Louisiana, was built in 1850 and is one of the largest extant plantations in the South. Its cotton pressing and ginning equipment includes this rare nineteenth-century "system" cotton gin. It is part of Cane River Creole National Historical Park.

banned in 1808—and cotton harvests increased. By 1860, North Carolina had more than 300,000 slaves. Cotton brought great prosperity to many Southern states, including Mississippi, which became one of the wealthiest after it joined the Union in 1817.

Cotton cultivation soon generated a demand for more arable land, pushing the South's frontier borders farther west. By 1820, Southerners were planting cotton in the Mississippi Valley, around Vicksburg and Natchez, and from Mobile to Tuscaloosa in Alabama. Due to the "removal acts" passed by Congress, Native Americans including the Creek, Chickasaw, and Choctaw were pushed off their land in Georgia, Alabama, and Mississippi and forced to resettle in Indian Territory (mainly Oklahoma). Their properties were seized by immigrant farmers from 1817–19, then again from 1834–37. Once former Native American land along the Gulf Coast was opened up to farming in the 1830s, cotton crops spread as far as Arkansas. By 1860, the Cotton, or Black, Belt also extended north into western Kentucky. The term "black belt" was coined later in the nineteenth century to refer to that broad region of the United States where African-Americans outnumbered other

ethnic groups at the time, in most if not all counties coinciding with the growth in cotton cultivation.

The South's plantation system thrived in the regions where cotton, sugarcane, and rice were grown. The big plantations operated predominantly on a principle of self-sufficiency, which entailed also growing beef and hogs, flour and hominy—even though using slaves to produce these foodstuffs for local consumption was not efficient. Many Southern states ended up buying meat and cereals from the upper Mississippi Valley. Most of the cotton harvested in the South's Black Belt traveled by steamboat to ports like New Orleans, Louisiana, and Charleston, South Carolina, for transport abroad. Cotton remained the chief U.S. export until the twentieth century.

When the War Between the States began, Confederate leaders mistakenly assumed England would support the Confederacy to ensure it kept its textile factories busy. Because slaves did most of the farm labor in the South, cotton stayed a relatively profitable crop during the Civil War despite Britain's lack of political support of the Confederacy, and Southerners remained adamant in their opposition to abolition.

Above: Green Hill Plantation in Campbell County, Virginia, is a particularly good example of Southern antebellum architecture. The oldest part of the main house is believed to have been built in 1797, while the nearby granary was constructed in 1821. Most of the L-shaped house was built later by Samuel Pannill.

Opposite: This Virginia tobacco field illustrates one of the state's most important crops. Tobacco growing dates back to the earliest settlers, and it was Virginia's first commercial crop. The colonists first tried (unsuccessfully) to produce silk, sassafras, glass, soap, lumber, pitch, and tar for export to England.

Below: This Tennessee farm is in the 6,800-acre valley named Cades Cove.

The havoc wreaked by the war did, however, depress cotton production until 1879. When the federal government failed to redistribute land in the South in the Reconstruction era, former slaves were forced to become sharecroppers. In most cases, they ended up no better off than before emancipation. By 1890, 60 percent of South Carolina's farmers were sharecroppers.

Other major crops in the South during the nineteenth century were corn, tobacco, sugarcane, rice, and indigo (source of the valuable blue dye). Corn, or maize, which had first been cultivated in Middle America, was a popular Native American crop, and settlers learned how to cultivate it from them. As early as 1631, Virginia was exporting corn. By the middle of the nineteenth century it became used predominantly to feed livestock and poultry. In the latter part of the century, wooden silos were used to store all parts of the corn plant, except the roots, to provide fodder. Virginia, Kentucky, and Tennessee led the country in corn production by 1839, but then the Corn Belt moved north and west, rapidly leaving them behind. Boiling corn mash to make liquor for sale or home use was common, particularly in Kentucky and Virginia. Bourbon is the Kentucky-created whiskey blend made out of corn mash that has been produced in that state for over 200 years. Heaven Hill, a giant distilling plant near Bardstown, Kentucky, today offers tours of its plant, where some twenty-five million barrels of bourbon are processed.

STEMMERY.

TOBACCO FACTORY.

DAVID DUNLOP

Tobacco developed as a cash crop in Virginia almost as soon as the region was colonized, then expanded into North Carolina and Kentucky around the end of the eighteenth century. North Carolina now produces half the nation's cigarettes, as well as a great deal of its pipe and chewing tobacco. The practice of smoking or chewing tobacco began with Native Americans who used dried, crushed tobacco leaves socially and in their ceremonies. The addictive habit quickly spread, first to Europe and then the rest of the world. All too often, early tobacco farmers planted their crops continuously, creating a receptive climate for insect and parasite infection, as well as depleting and eroding the soil. This practice spurred landowners to look for fresh soil farther west in the Piedmont region and beyond the Appalachians.

After the Civil War, tobacco kept the Virginia economy going in the midst of economic devastation. Richard Joshua Reynolds, from Patrick County, Virginia, traded tobacco in that state, then founded R. J. Reynolds Tobacco in North Carolina. North Carolina's Washington Duke started growing tobacco in 1850, using borrowed slave labor. Duke's son Brodie started a tobacco plant in Durham, and when Brodie's brothers Benjamin and James Buchanan joined him, they acquired a cigarette-making machine that cut production costs in half. James A. Bonsack of Lynchburg, Virginia, invented the cigarette machine in 1880. Richmond, Virginia, is still the site of Universal Corporation, the world's largest independent tobacco-leaf seller.

Sugarcane cultivation proliferated in Louisiana along the lower Mississippi River, and rice was grown along the coasts of South Carolina and Georgia. Virginian Cyrus McCormick's invention of the reaper in 1831 revolutionized the harvesting of grains. McCormick's home and workshop near Lexington continue to attract large numbers of visitors. The peanut also has its place in Southern history. George Washington Carver became one of Alabama's most famous African-Americans because of his turn-of-the-century research on crop rotation and peanuts. Discovering 325 different uses for the popular nut, Carver is known as the father of the peanut industry, Georgia's largest cash crop. Today it is a $2 billion a year industry.

As early as the 1840s, Virginia farmers became important suppliers of the nation's fresh fruits and vegetables, and the truck farming business there continued to thrive after the War Between the States because it wasn't dependent on slave labor. Florida's citrus industry dates back to Christopher Columbus. The original trees that bore oranges and lemons were found in Asia—China, Southeast Asia, and probably India—and their cultivation had begun in prehistoric times. By the Middle Ages the fruits appeared in southern Europe. Columbus brought orange seeds (along with lemon and citron seeds) to Haiti in 1493, and the early Spanish explorers imported them to the Sunshine State. Seventy years later, St. Augustine's founder Pedro Menéndez de Avilés described citrus trees growing wild around that city. Oranges were introduced as a commercial crop in Pinellas County around 1800 and grapefruit followed in 1825. Florida leads the world in production of grapefruit, and only Brazil outproduces Florida in oranges. Florida physician John Gorrie helped to boost the state's citrus business through his pioneering work in ice-making, refrigeration, and air conditioning, beginning with the invention of an air-cooling machine for his patients. He received a patent for his invention in 1851.

Opposite: T. B. Williams Tobacco Company (above) in Virginia was one of the early manufacturers of tobacco products and employed many African-Americans. The first American cigarette factory opened in 1864. David Dunlop's tobacco factory (below), dating back to the early 1800s, was one of Petersburg, Virginia's most successful antebellum businesses.

Overleaf: Snow-covered farmland in Avery County near Banner Elk, western North Carolina, frames the landscape in the Blue Ridge Mountains. The eastern part of North Carolina was swampland until it was developed for agriculture beginning in the late eighteenth century.

Left: George Washington Carver, born to slaves in Missouri, taught at Tuskegee Institute in Alabama for most of his life. He developed a crop rotation system for cotton and legumes to keep the soil from becoming depleted.

Above: Churchill Downs Racetrack, home of the Kentucky Derby, dates back to 1874, when it was established by Colonel M. Lewis Clark. Horse racing has been a part of Kentucky's history since 1789.

Below: Avery Island, Louisiana, is home to rock salt mines. This product, known as halite, is used today to de-ice highways.

In 1874, Georgia became the first state in the nation to create a Department of Agriculture. Pecans and peaches are two well-known Georgia crops in addition to peanuts. Probably the most famous consumable produced in Georgia, though, is Coca-Cola. James Pemberton is credited with inventing the carbonated drink, mixing it up in the backyard of his Marietta, Georgia, home. "Coke" was sold for the first time at Jacob's Pharmacy on May 8, 1886, in Atlanta. By the end of the century, Coca-Cola had become the nation's most popular drink.

After the Civil War, Kentucky's lush bluegrass attracted thoroughbred horse breeders, an occupation based during colonial times in Virginia. Horse farms proliferated around Lexington. Banker Lewis Clark built Churchill Downs Racetrack outside Louisville and inaugurated the Kentucky Derby in 1875. That year Aristides, an undersized, three-year-old chestnut colt, won the race at Churchill Downs. He was ridden by an African-American jockey named Oliver Lewis, who heads the list of the Derby's first thirteen jockey winners, all of whom were African-American. Later in 1917, Lexington-born Man O' War won twenty races, becoming the most famous horse in racing. The Kentucky Derby, held annually in April, became the most celebrated horse race in the nation.

Mineral resources played a role—if a less significant one than agriculture—in the South's nineteenth-century history. Salt mines date back as far as the seventeenth century in Jamestown, Virginia, where colonists set up a solar saltworks on Smith's Island. West Virginia, particularly in Marshall County, followed in the nineteenth century as a producer of "white gold," as salt has been called. Glassmaking in America was another early industry, starting in 1608 when Captain John Smith's London Company opened up for business at Glasshouse Point in Jamestown, Virginia.

After the son of North Carolina farmer John Reed discovered a gold nugget outside of Charlotte in 1799, Reed sold the seventeen-pound stone to a jeweler for $3.50, unaware of its worth. In 1803, Reed formed a prospecting partnership with three other men, and they unearthed a twenty-eight-pound gold nugget. Their discovery started the nation's first gold rush, establishing a $1-million industry in North Carolina. It subsided once gold was found in California in 1848 and ended altogether after the Civil War. Reed Gold Mine in Midland, North Carolina, has since become a historic site.

Birmingham and Bessemer, Alabama, have supplied hematite for iron and steel production in the northern part of that state since the nineteenth century. The La Belle Iron Works, a producer of nails in Wheeling, West Virginia, dates back to 1852. Steel sheets and tin were produced by the Wheeling manufacturer Whitaker-Gessner, beginning in 1875, and the Wheeling Corrugating Company started to produce roofing and siding in 1890.

Coal ore underlies much of West Virginia and Kentucky. There are sixty-two workable bituminous coal seams in West Virginia alone. Coal mining began there in 1810 outside of Wheeling. For most of the nineteenth century, West Virginia's coal was confined to domestic use, since only the ore retrieved from those mines near navigable rivers could be exported. By 1883, though, the state acquired adequate railroad coverage, and production leapt to three million tons. Only Wyoming and Kentucky produce more coal than West Virginia. In Kentucky, coal is found in the Western Coal Fields and the mountainous eastern part of the state. Southwestern Virginia also has coal mines, and once the Norfolk & Western Railroad built rail lines there in 1882, it could be transported to Norfolk. Coal also began to be mined in the East Tennessee mountains during the nineteenth century. Alabama began to develop coal mines like Warrior Field in the northern part of the state, thanks to the arrival of railroads.

The South is home to many other natural resources. Elberton, Georgia, is Granite Capital of the World with forty-five granite quarries. In Alabama, marble began to be mined in the Piedmont region in the nineteenth century. Kennesaw, Georgia, is home to the

Below: Gantts Marble Quarry is located in Talladega County, Alabama. Marble has been quarried in Alabama since 1840, and the state is a leading supplier of the stone. The quarry is owned by Georgia Marble Company.

Georgia Marble Company, the world's largest marble producer and site of the largest open-pit quarry in the world. The Lincoln Memorial is made of Georgia marble. The west coast of Florida provides 80 percent of the United States' phosphate, most of which becomes fertilizer. Natural gas is a natural resource produced in the western sections of West Virginia, and Wheeling acquired the Virginia colony's first chartered gas company in 1850. Limestone is quarried in the eastern part of the state. After bauxite, used in aluminum, was discovered near Little Rock, Arkansas's population tripled between 1870 and 1900.

Oil emerged as another new industry for the South in the nineteenth century, encouraging the growth of new towns and the commerce they generated. Alabama has petroleum resources, particularly in the southwest section of the state and offshore. Florida has oil wells in Santa Rosa County, and it produces fuller's earth, a substance used to process petroleum. Other chemical products in Alabama, besides oil, include fertilizers, insecticides, chemically produced fibers like rayon, and other industrial chemicals.

The hard times that followed the Civil War spurred the introduction of industrialization across the South. Construction of large, centrally located sugarcane refineries in Louisiana, for example, allowed landowners there to share the cost of capitalization. Duncan Kenner, who founded the Louisiana Sugar Planters Association, helped cut labor costs by introducing the use of movable railroad tracks. After one field had been harvested, the railroad tracks were dismantled and moved to another harvest location.

Left: Alabama's Cheaha Mountain is located in Talladega National Forest. The area is rich in coal and iron deposits, and the center of state's nineteenth-century mining industry was nearby in Anniston and Birmingham. Cheaha, the word for "high place" in the Creek language, is the highest point in Alabama at 2,407 feet. Cheaha Mountain State Park is one of the oldest parks in Alabama.

Right: *Two millstones at the nineteenth-century Mingus Flour Mill, located in Great Smoky Mountains National Park in Cherokee, North Carolina.*

Below: *This vintage steam locomotive from the Norfolk Southern Railroad makes its home in the Ernest Norris Railroad Yards in Alabama. Norfolk Southern has more than 14,000 miles of track in twenty states, including all of the Southern states except Arkansas.*

South Carolina had built fifty textile mills by 1892. Most of them were built in the northern part of the state on rivers that could supply electricity. Lumber, iron, steel, and flour mills helped industrialize Tennessee. Textile mills also appeared in Nashville, Knoxville, and Jackson, Tennessee. In North Carolina, lumber supported a burgeoning furniture industry, and in Alabama, manufacture of paper and pulp ultimately became the state's biggest product, with mills in Mobile, Montgomery, and Childersburg.

Railroad construction supplied a central component to industrialization and economic development in the South. The longest railroad line then in the world was opened in South Carolina in 1833. It ran 136 miles between Charleston and Aiken. Norfolk Southern opened an eight-mile line between Petersburg and Hopewell, Virginia, in 1838 and continues to operate out of Norfolk. A boom

in railroad building opened up large sections of northern and western Louisiana, and Arkansas, to economic development. After the railroads arrived, the lumber companies stripped Louisiana of its pinewoods. Then the land was sold cheaply, often to immigrant farmers. Louisiana's Italian immigrants, for instance, planted strawberries. In South Carolina, railroad lines doubled in length between 1877 and 1900. In Arkansas new railroads in the nineteenth century transported lumber and coal.

The Civil War destroyed most of the South's existing railroad lines. Their reconstruction took years, and Virginia's ports played an important role in the post-Civil War years. Norfolk developed into a major port for the export of cotton. Nearby Danville has been the home of Dan River Cotton Mills, one of the largest in the world, since 1883. The Newport News Shipbuilding and Dry Dock Company, one of the world's largest, started in 1886. New Orleans's importance as a port city dates back into its earliest days. Today the Port of

New Orleans has twenty-two miles of facilities for loading and unloading products, controls eighty-eight miles of waterfront, and has fifty major docking areas. More than 2,500 ships use the city's port and 100,000 barges move through it annually.

The South's fishing industry is a small but important part of the region's economy. Louisiana and Alabama are known for their shrimp, and other Southern marine products include oysters, blue crabs, red snapper, catfish, and mussels. In addition to shrimp, Florida supplies the nation with lobsters, scallops, grouper, and mackerel. Although Maryland is better known for its crabs, Virginia's "watermen" also ply the Chesapeake Bay for this delicacy.

The plantation system and the antebellum Southern way of life—which is still often romanticized—was transformed by the Civil War. The latter half of the nineteenth century will be remembered as the time when the South rebuilt its economy and readied itself to enter the modern world.

Overleaf: The Cape Hatteras Lighthouse on the Outer Banks of North Carolina was moved some 2,900 feet inland in 1999 because it was being undermined by beach erosion.

Below: The roundhouse and work buildings of the Baltimore & Ohio railroad yard in Martinsburg, West Virginia, were rebuilt after the Civil War. Martinsburg was created by the railroad company after it decided to cross into Virginia at Harpers Ferry instead of Hagerstown, Maryland, so it could reach the Ohio River.

SHAPING
THE
MODERN WORLD

Previous page: A New Orleans French Quarter balcony with mask decoration during Mardi Gras, which means "Fat Tuesday." The popular carnival dates back to the French tradition of slaughtering a fatted cow on the last Tuesday before Lent.

The South had experienced profound changes during the nineteenth century, the most important of which were the end of slavery and consequent changes in the South's economy. The dawn of a new century, however, did not bring an immediate round of dramatic change. In 1896 the U.S. Supreme Court gave a green light to continued segregation with its "separate but equal" ruling. In 1900, due to Jim Crow laws, African-Americans still could not sit with white passengers on trains (and later on buses). They had to use separate rest rooms, go to separate schools, and eat and sleep in separate restaurants and hotels. Miscegenation—marriage between the races—was still a crime.

After Alabama passed a new constitution in 1901, only 5 percent of the eligible African-American population could vote. Limitations on their voting included establishment of a poll tax, proof of literacy, and often proof of solvency or land ownership. In South Carolina, the per-pupil state subsidy for white schools was $8 in 1907, while for black schools it was $1.57. Virginia passed legislation determining who was a Negro—as African-Americans were called then—and who was not. After the Civil War, Virginia law decreed that anyone with one quarter Negro blood would be considered black. In 1910 the fraction was decreased to one-sixteenth thereby assigning even more people to a life of segregation.

But increasing numbers of African-Americans began to overcome these barriers. One such was journalist Ida Bell Wells. Born a slave in Mississippi, she edited the *Memphis Free Speech* in Tennessee, attacking segregation. In 1909 she also helped found the National Association for the Advancement of Colored People, or NAACP.

The early years of the century saw many Southerners achieve national celebrity. Virginia native Woodrow Wilson was elected the country's eighth president in 1912 and won re-election in 1916. Although he did not succeed in getting the United States to join the League of Nations after World War I, the United

Right: During the Depression years, African-Americans throughout the South were segregated in public facilities like this streetcar terminal.

States would eventually join its successor, the United Nations. Juliette Gordon Low of Savannah, Georgia, created the Girl Scouts of America in 1912. Ironically, Georgia later became the first state to turn down the 19th amendment to the Constitution, allowing women to vote, although it passed anyway.

Much of the South remained agrarian well into the twentieth century. Arkansas farmer William Fuller planted that state's first major rice crop in 1904, and rice became a major agricultural resource there. Between 1904 and 1927, much of Louisiana's woodlands were clear-cut. Pine forests cut down by lumber companies were, however, replanted or turned into vegetable and grain fields.

Making its way up from Mexico and across Texas, an insect plague—the boll weevil—hit Alabama's cotton crops in 1913 and spread rapidly through the South in the 1920s. South Carolina lost half its cotton crop to the boll weevil, a beetle whose larvae eat the plant. In Georgia, cotton harvests plummeted from 2,122,000 bales in 1918 to 388,000 in 1923. Resourceful farmers diversified, planting tobacco and wheat instead of cotton in South Carolina and peanuts in Alabama. In fact, in 1919 a statue was erected in Enterprise, Alabama, to honor the boll weevil for forcing farmers to diversify their crops.

In 1924, Georgia's first crop duster planes, owned by Huff-Daland Dusters of Macon, put an end to the blight. When Collett Woolman bought the business in 1928, it moved to Atlanta and became Delta Airlines. William Berry Hartsfield—later Atlanta's mayor—had already begun to turn an abandoned Atlanta racetrack called Candler Field into an international airport.

Turn-of-the-century strife in the South was not always race-based. In 1904, Kentucky's Black Patch farmers in the western part of the state refused to sell their tobacco at deflated prices to the American Tobacco Company. The giant tobacco concern offered higher prices to farmers who ignored the boycott. That led to beatings and crop and warehouse burnings for four years. Yet Kentucky remains second only to North Carolina in tobacco farming, and the small rural farm continued to play an important role in Kentucky's economy through the 1950s and beyond.

Symbolic of the South's turn toward industry in the twentieth century was Wilbur and Orville Wright's experiments with flying in North Carolina. In 1901 and 1902, they flew gliders from the sand dunes of the Outer Banks. Their first powered airplane flight took place on December 17, 1903, between Kitty Hawk and Nag's Neck.

Above: Airplane pioneer Orville Wright recorded the moment of lift-off with his camera. His brother Wilbur was piloting the world's first plane flight at Kitty Hawk, North Carolina, on December 17, 1903.

Overleaf: Swann Covered Bridge (also called the Joy Bridge) crosses the Locust Fork River in Blount County, Alabama. Built in 1933, it is the ninth-longest covered bridge in the country and the longest one in the state, spanning over 324 feet. Alabama receives more annual rainfall than any other state, and its rivers regularly flood.

By 1900 West Virginia was producing 21 million tons of coal annually, and the state's economy was controlled by the coal industry. African-Americans and European immigrants flocked to the state for employment in the coal mines. The mining companies used many unscrupulous practices to cheat their workers, like paying them with scrip usable only in company stores that sold overpriced goods. Miners lost wages through cribbing—when the company used larger coal cars than the specified size on which workers' wages were based. Safety at work was another issue. Monongah, West Virginia, experienced one of the worst coal-mining accidents in the nation on December 6, 1907, when 361 miners died.

The United Mine Workers of America ran into frequent roadblocks attempting to unionize West Virginia's mines. Although the UMWA succeeded in starting a union at the Kanawha-New River Coalfield in 1902, the owners brought in private detectives to harass the workers. Irish-born Mary Harris "Mother" Jones led the way in unionizing West Virginia. In 1913 the level of violence grew so high that Governor William E. Glasscock declared martial law. Newly elected Governor Henry D. Hatfield dictated a settlement of the Paint Creek strike that included a nine-hour workday and the elimination of company store control. Director John Sayles's film *Matewan* memorializes the fight to unionize in Mingo County. Not

Below: *Kaymoor Coal Mine in Kaymoor, West Virginia, was one of a number of mines in the New River Gorge section of the state where boom towns appeared in the early part of the twentieth century. Kaymoor One produced almost 17 million tons of coal during its more than sixty years of operation.*

Left: U.S. Steel first set up shop in Alabama in 1907. Pictured here is a period photo of the U.S. Steel Fairfield Works, which has been in operation since 1897. The steel factory was set up here because of its accessibility by rail, barge, and highway.

until 1933 did federal law protect union rights, and the unionization of the southern coalfields could proceed.

With foundries already a thriving industry, U.S. Steel, the largest such company in the nation, arrived in Alabama in 1907. North Carolina's textile mills became that state's biggest employers, hiring children and "rednecks"—farmers turned factory workers with red clay dust still covering their necks. Two crystals found by John Huddleston on his Arkansas farm in 1906 turned out to be diamonds. Huddleston then proceeded to build the nation's only diamond mine. In 1909, Sulphur, Louisiana, became the site for extensive sulphur mining.

After oil was discovered there in 1901, Louisiana became the third largest U.S. refiner, and the state produces one quarter of American petrochemicals. The need to transport oil from Texas and Oklahoma to the port of Baton Rouge brought new pipelines through Louisiana starting in 1910. The oil boom led to the age of the automobile. Louisiana's Governor John M. Parker oversaw construction of a highway system for the state. The new roads helped Louisiana dig out after the Great Mississippi Flood of 1927, and comprehensive flood control projects followed. North Carolina developed such an active road-building program it became known as the Good Road State.

Above: *The Shelborne Hotel on Collins Avenue in Miami Beach, Florida, typifies the Art Deco style popular in the 1920s and '30s. It was characterized by pastel colors, streamlined rectilinear shapes, and a clean-cut idealism.*

Opposite: *Paurotis palms and mahogany hammock at Everglades, Florida, one of the world's most remarkable wetlands environments. Draining it for land reclamation started as early as 1908, but recently there has been an effort to allow water back into some of the area.*

Florida became the first of the Southern states to experience a boom in tourism. Starting in the early 1900s, affluent Northerners flocked to the Sunshine State on vacations. Governor Napoleon B. Broward responded by initiating land reclamation. He oversaw construction of a canal system that drained the Everglades to allow for home construction. Automobile entrepreneur Carl Fisher turned Miami Beach into a resort by draining its mangrove swamps. By the 1920s the advent of the automobile made southern Florida even more popular. In four years Miami quadrupled its population.

Many other Southern states began to discover that tourism was a boon to their economies. Nashville, Tennessee's Grand Ole Opry, a country music center, attracted tourists from its opening in 1925. Tennessee's Lost Sea Caverns, containing one of the largest underground lakes in the world, and Great Smoky Mountains National Park, com-

missioned in 1926, also attracted tourists. Arkansas's Hot Springs became part of the National Park system in 1921, the only city-based national park.

The United States entered World War I in 1914, and the South geared up to help. Alvin C. York of Pall Mall, Tennessee, came to symbolize American heroism, after capturing enemy troops in a 1918 battle despite being grossly outnumbered. He became one of the most decorated American soldiers of World War I. Camp Shelby near Hattiesburg, Mississippi, was the site for one of the U.S. Army's major training operations, and Fort Knox in Kentucky was another. At West Point, Mississippi, one of the first military flight schools, Payne Field, trained fighter pilots. Charleston's Navy Yard built coal-burning destroyers to aid the war effort.

Lack of economic opportunities led many African-Americans to leave Mississippi, Virginia, and South Carolina during World War I. They

Above: This World War I wagon was put into service to distribute conservation posters from the Federal Food Administration in Mobile, Alabama. The FFA, a predecessor to the FDA, was set up in 1917, and it had power to fix food prices, oversee exports, and act against hoarding and profiteering.

migrated north to take factory jobs given up by soldiers. By 1930, African-Americans in South Carolina were outnumbered for the first time since before the Civil War.

Alabama's steel mills ran twenty-four hours a day to keep up with the war demand, and they often leased convicts to mine the ore, a practice finally outlawed in 1928. Mobile's shipyard was also kept busy. Two nitrate processing plants and Wilson Dam were built in Muscle Shoals to provide materials for explosives. In Georgia, the popularity of tufted chenille bedspreads made by Catherine Evans Whitener sparked a cottage industry involving as many as 10,000 women working at home by World War I. U.S. Highway 41 between Dalton and Cartersville acquired a new name—Bedspread Boulevard.

The post-World War I years led to an increase in violence against African-Americans in the South. In Rosewood, Florida, a mob of 200 burned that black community to the ground in 1923. Rosewood's story is memorialized in a 1997 film of the same name by John Singleton. Labor unrest plagued the

1920s and 1930s in Kentucky, where coal miners in "Bloody Harlan," as that county was known, struggled to unionize and fought for better wages.

After oil was discovered in 1921, 500 wells went into operation in El Dorado, Arkansas. By 1924 Arkansas became the nation's fourth biggest oil-producing state. Farm workers left Arkansas in droves, though, in search of jobs as machines replaced them.

In 1925, after Tennessee outlawed the teaching of evolution in public schools, the famous "Monkey Trial" took place in Dayton. Celebrated lawyer Clarence Darrow defended John Scopes for teaching evolution, but William Jennings Bryan, the "silver-tongued orator," won the case. Evolution was not taught again in Tennessee until 1967.

In a prelude to the Great Depression, Florida's inflated real estate values began to plummet in 1926. Devastating hurricanes hit south Florida in 1926 and 1928, furthering the economic downturn. The Mississippi River flooded the Delta in 1927, leaving 100,000 homeless in Mississippi and up to 300,000 in Louisiana. In 1929, the Alabama-Tombigbee Rivers flooded southern Alabama, causing $6 million in damage. That same year, a Mediterranean fruit fly infestation killed off 60 percent of Florida's citrus crops. Still Florida's population soared, as northerners migrated south to buy and develop the state's now-cheap land. By 1935, Florida had opened up nine parks for tourists and Floridians alike.

The Depression brought bankruptcy for Arkansas farmers, and many of its factories closed their doors. In South Carolina, those factory workers who were able to hang onto their jobs saw their salaries drop to ten cents an hour. President Franklin D. Roosevelt's New Deal helped bail out the South. One of the best-known New Deal projects was the Tennessee Valley Authority. Starting in 1933, the TVA built dams along the Tennessee River and its tributaries to control flooding and bring electricity to the state.

The Civilian Conservation Corps and Works Progress Administration hired 70,000 Alabamians to build new roads, government buildings, and parks. Mississippi's Governor Hugh White established a program called Balance Agriculture with Industry, introducing mechanized farming and electricity to many parts of the state. One famous New Deal project in Virginia was construction of the scenic Skyline Drive. The scenic Blue Ridge Parkway meanders along the crest line of North Carolina's Blue Ridge Mountains,

thanks to a 1935 New Deal Civilian Conservation Corps project. In 1936, the U.S. Treasury established Kentucky's Fort Knox as the repository for its gold reserves, bringing jobs to that state.

The Kingfish, as Louisiana's colorful governor from 1928 to 1932—Huey Long—was called, built a 4.4-mile bridge across the Mississippi that was completed in 1935 and considered an engineering marvel at the time. He supported education and abolished the poll tax, first as governor and later as a U.S. senator. A controversial figure, Long was murdered by a political opponent in 1935.

The bombing of Pearl Harbor on December 7, 1941, and the subsequent U.S. declaration of war brought profound changes to the South. Unemployment dropped in most Southern states when American industries geared up for war production. Tennessee's Oak Ridge National Laboratory came into

Below: The U.S. Naval Air Station at Banana River, Florida, housed planes like this one during World War II. The aircraft were used for anti-submarine patrols along the Florida coast.

Above: *Beach and surf create a scenic tourist attraction at Cape Canaveral National Seashore near New Smyrna, Florida. This National Seashore consists of 24 miles of undeveloped beach, the longest such area on Florida's east coast. It is owned by Kennedy Space Center, created in 1955.*

Opposite, above: *A 1941 scene from the collection of the Office of War Information showing an overhead crane and ships under construction at the shipyards in Newport News, Virginia.*

existence in 1942, one of three sites established for the development of the atomic bomb. Chuck Yeager from Myra, West Virginia, who as a test pilot later became the first person to break the sound barrier, flew sixty-four missions as a fighter pilot. Virginia provided homes for a wartime influx of government workers and offices. Kentucky's industries offered jobs to both African-Americans and women in unprecedented numbers.

Soldiers trained at Georgia's Fort Stewart, Fort Benning, and Fort Gordon, while Marines went to South Carolina's Parris Island. World War II changed Georgia's economy into an industrially based one. In 1941 Warner Robins Air Force Base and Air Logistics Center were built outside of Macon, and together they have become the state's largest employer. Kentucky's Fort Knox and Camp Breckinridge by Morganfield also trained many soldiers. The Ford Motor Company plant in

Louisville manufactured a total of 93,389 Army jeeps, and munitions were made in a Paducah plant.

Georgia's ports played an active role in the war. Savannah shipped the most weapons to Europe of any U.S. harbor, and the Brunswick Shipyards built ninety-nine of the Liberty ships carrying supplies to European allies. In one remarkable month, they produced seven of the ships. Louisiana's shipbuilding industry, as well as its military bases, also supported the nation's war effort. During the war, the sea lanes off North Carolina's Outer Banks were dubbed Torpedo Alley because of the German submarines that staged ship attacks there. Alabama factories helped lift the state out of Depression doldrums by producing $500 million in wartime products. The war also helped end sharecropping in Alabama, as farmers migrated to Birmingham, Huntsville, and Mobile's factories. The Tuskegee Airmen, a celebrated group

of African-American fighter pilots, trained at Tuskegee Army Air Field.

In a post-World War II slump, West Virginia's coal mines produced one-third of what they had during the war. Ex-coal miners left to find jobs in cities like Detroit, Chicago, or Cleveland. In South Carolina, the federally funded Santee Cooper hydroelectric plant opened in 1941 and spurred post-World War II economic growth there. The Atomic Energy Commission's Savannah River Plant was built in 1950 to make atomic bombs. That same year, the former German aerospace engineer Wernher von Braun was assigned to develop rocket technology at Redstone Arsenal in Huntsville, Alabama.

Southern shipping got a boost when the Gulf Intracoastal Waterway was completed in 1949. Over 1,000 miles long, it connects Carabelle, Florida, with Alabama, Mississippi, Louisiana, and Texas. Cape Canaveral, Florida, opened in 1950, as a U.S. Air Force missile test-

ing facility. Virginia remained an important ship-building center, and the first of the giant supercarriers, the mighty U.S.S. *Forrestal*, was launched December 11, 1954, from the Newport News Shipbuilding and Dry Dock Company. The S.S. *United States*, the last U.S. passenger superliner, left Newport News on its maiden voyage to Southampton, England on July 3, 1952. The 1950s in Mississippi saw the clothing industry surpass lumber as the state's biggest manufacturing industry.

Below: These men were photographed in an isolated part of Kentucky in 1940 carrying a coffin to the family graveyard. Marion Post Wolcott captured the scene as part of her series of documentary images of the Depression era for the Farm Security Administration.

Like many other Southern states, West Virginia developed its service industries during the postwar years. The biggest industry in many Southern states, though, became tourism. West Virginia's white-water rafting, ski slopes, fishing, hunting, caving, and rock climbing began to attract tourists. Virginia's beaches also drew tourists, particularly at Virginia Beach and Chincoteague, made famous by the wild horses written about in the children's book *Misty of Chincoteague*. Alabama offers tourists spectacular caves in the Appalachian Mountain system. Construction on Mississippi's Natchez Trace Parkway began in the 1930s, and it has become one of the state's big tourist attractions, along with Gulf Islands National Seashore and the Vicksburg National Military Park, which dates back to 1899. The Kentucky Highland Museum in Ashland attracts tourists to a state that earns $7 billion in tourism. Nashville and Memphis, Tennessee, draw tourists to their country music centers.

For millions of American children Walt Disney World's Magic Kingdom in Orlando, Florida, is a mecca. A variety of imaginary "worlds" have been created there, including Adventureland, Fantasyland, Tomorrowland, and Main Street U.S.A. St. Petersburg on Florida's west coast boasts the Salvador Dali Museum, and Sarasota features the Ringling Brothers Museum. Florida is also home to the nation's only remaining live coral reef at John Pennecamp Coral Reef State Park.

New Orleans, Louisiana, one of the country's oldest and most cosmopolitan cities, contributes to the state's tourism industry. The French Quarter is where Mardi Gras takes place, a pre-Lenten celebration in February. A temporary king is selected, and secret societies help organize some of the many festive events.

In 1954 the U.S. Supreme Court mandated desegregation of all public schools. Much of the South resisted the court decision, and in states like Virginia many

Right: The Grand Ole Opry in Nashville, Tennessee, is home to the oldest live radio show in the nation, broadcasting for over seventy years. The Opry has been located at a number of different sites, the most famous of which is the Ryman Auditorium, built in 1892. Many of the nation's most celebrated country singers have performed there over the years.

Left: This photograph of Martin Luther King, Jr., in a classroom at Tennessee's Highlander Folk School was used to discredit the pastor and civil rights leader during an era in which the spread of Communism was feared. King's inspired oratory and passionate commitment to peaceful protest in the cause of civil rights ultimately made him one of the twentieth century's most important figures.

parents put their children in private schools rather than send them to mixed schools. Kentucky became the first Southern state to follow the federal dictate to desegregate its schools. The University of Kentucky, perhaps in response to the demand for higher education by war veterans, began opening its doors to African-Americans as early as 1948.

Although conflicts over race relations plagued the South well into the mid-twentieth century, the region began to grow beyond the limitations of that deeply imbedded cultural problem. Many of the nation's greatest Americans were born and grew up in the South during that period. The most important civil rights leader in the nation, Martin Luther King, Jr., was born in Atlanta. Serving as pastor of the Dexter Avenue Baptist Church of Montgomery, Alabama, he founded the Southern Christian Leadership Conference in 1957. SCLC had its roots in the Montgomery Bus Boycott of 1955–6. A courageous African-American woman named Rosa Parks refused to give up her bus seat to a white man and was arrested, precipitating the 381-day boycott that launched the legendary civil rights movement of the 1960s.

One of the United States' greatest World War II heroes, General Douglas MacArthur, came from Little Rock, Arkansas. Elvis Presley, the self-styled "king of rock and roll," was born in Tupelo, Mississippi, and lived in Memphis, Tennessee. Other celebrated popular musicians who hail from the South are Leontyne Price, Ella Fitzgerald, Louis Armstrong, and William Warfield.

The South is celebrated for its great writers, who include Virginia-born novelist William Styron, author of *The Confessions of Nat Turner* and *Sophie's Choice*, the poet and memoirist Maya Angelou, Mississippian William Faulkner, Richard Wright, Eudora Welty, Tennessee Williams, Margaret Mitchell, Flannery O'Connor, Robert Penn Warren, and too many more to name.

By the mid-1900s the South no longer dwelled on outdated customs. If the region still had far to go in improving race relations, it would soon put the darkest chapters of its history behind it and concentrate on the best elements in its genteel traditions. The modern South welcomes tourists and industry alike, and offers the rest of the nation and the world an easygoing lifestyle redolent with charm.

Overleaf: This cherub fountain and lush, leafy garden are characteristic of Charleston, South Carolina, a city founded in 1670 as the capital of Carolina Colony. Entire districts of its eighteenth- and nineteenth-century buildings have been preserved.

KENTUCKY, WEST VIRGINIA, AND VIRGINIA

KENTUCKY: THE EAST

Frankfort

Kentucky State Capitol: An impressive structure with Greek and Roman architectural elements, completed in 1909. Its 70 Ionic columns and carved sculpture are impressive, and the interior of the building is equally elegant. The *Floral Clock* in the park measures 34 feet in diameter and features around 20,000 flowers on its face. Next to the Capitol is the *Kentucky Governor's Mansion*, a Beaux-Arts structure from 1914.

Kentucky Military History Museum: Located in the former Kentucky State Arsenal, a castellated Gothic Revival building from 1850

Liberty Hall Historic Site: Georgian mansion built by John Brown, Kentucky's first U.S. senator, in the 1790s. The house is furnished with family pieces and includes a large library. The site also features the *Orlando Brown House*, dating from 1835, and newly restored formal gardens.

Harrodsburg

Old Fort Harrod State Park: Replica of the 1774 log fort used by early settlers as protection against Native American attacks. The site also includes a *Pioneer Cemetery.*

Shaker Village of Pleasant Hill: The largest and most complete historic village of its kind in the United States, containing 33 original 19th-century buildings with a large collection of furniture, tools, and other items.

Lexington

Kentucky Horse Park: Theme park that honors the animal for which the Bluegrass Country has become famous. The visitor center features a film show, and the park also contains the *Man o' War Monument*, the *International Museum of the Horse*, self-guided farm tours, and presentations of the park's 40 breeds.

Middlesboro

Cumberland Gap National Historic Park: **See Middlesboro, East Tennessee.**

Richmond

Fort Boonesborough State Park: Historic fort built by David Boone in the 1770s on the site of a severe Native American attack in 1778. The site features a museum, as well as reproductions of blockhouses and cabins, and costumed interpreters demonstrate craft-making and pioneer life.

Union

Big Bone Lick State Park: Ancient salt lick and sulfur spring, where the scattered bones of a large number of prehistoric animals were found. The park museum exhibits many of the artifacts.

KENTUCKY: THE WEST

Fort Knox

The site of the *U.S. Gold Depository,* stored in the Gold Bullion Depository building and surrounded by high-security measures.

Hodgenville

Abraham Lincoln Birthplace National Historic Site: A neoclassical marble monument houses the restored cabin at the site of Lincoln's birth.

Louisville

Churchill Downs: Historical race track and the site of Kentucky's first derby in 1875. Adjacent is the *Kentucky Derby Museum.*

Mammoth Cave National Park

With 350 miles of explored passageways, this is the longest recorded cave system in the world. Many artifacts of its former inhabitants have been found, dating from 2500 B.C. to year 0, some bearing evidence of cannibalism. Tours of varying length are operated, including a five-mile hike/crawl through unimproved passageways. Nearby are various smaller caves, including the *Crystal Onyx Cave,* and *Hidden River Cave,* to which the very rare blind cavefish has returned.

Shelbyville

Bluegrass Bison Ranch: This 1,000-acre working "Wild West" ranch, complete with herds of buffalo, features original 18th-century buildings and explores the history of the bison and frontier life.

WEST VIRGINIA: THE EASTERN PANHANDLE AND THE POTOMAC HIGHLANDS

Berkeley Springs

Home of America's first spa, historic Berkeley Springs has attracted visitors for two centuries. Today, visitors can choose between the historic spas in the *Berkeley Springs State Park* and the contemporary spas.

Cass

Cass Scenic Railroad State Park: This historic railroad takes visitors back to the era when West Virginia's timber industry was powered by steam trains. Visitors can ride through the beautiful wilderness in an original Shay locomotive. The area also contains many restored company buildings.

Harpers Ferry National Historic Park

This area has hosted events crucial to the Civil War, the history of industry and transportation, and Native American and African American history. The abolitionist John Brown was captured here. Attractions include the *Lower Town Historic District*, with many restored 19th-century buildings and museums; the *Maryland Heights*, a rewarding hike passing ruins of many Civil War fortifications; and *Virginius Island*, a prosperous industrial community devastated by the Civil War and by flooding.

Hillsboro

Droop Mountain Battlefield State Park: Site of the largest Civil War battle in West Virginia. Part of the battlefield is restored and marked for visitors; also features a small museum with Civil War artifacts.

Riverton

Seneca Caverns: The largest caverns in the state, rediscovered in 1760.

WEST VIRGINIA: THE NORTH

Fairmont

Pricketts Fort State Park: Built in 1774, the fort originally provided refuge for the early settlers and frontiersmen against attacks by Native Americans; has now been reconstructed and features living history interpretations and craft demonstrations, and includes the listed *Job Prickett House.*

Moundsville

Grave Creek Mound Historic Site: The largest of the conical mounds, built by the Adena people approximately 2,000 years ago.

Prabhupada's Palace of Gold: Built by Srila Prabhupada, a poor Indian and a strong devotee of Krishna who came to America and established the International Society for Krishna Consciousness. The palace (built by his devotees, under Srila's guidance) is a showplace of Asian splendor.

Parkersburg

Blennerhassett Island Historical Park: The reconstructed mansion of the area's most controversial character, Harmann Blennerhassett. Crafts are demonstrated on the site, and visitors can ride around the island in horse-drawn wagons or visit the *Blennerhassett Museum.*

Weston

Jackson's Mill Historic Area: Operating water-powered gristmill, built in 1841 by Cummins Jackson. The site also includes a blacksmith shop, several cabins, and *Jackson's Mill Museum.*

Wheeling

West Virginia Independence Hall: Renaissance Revival structure, from 1859, that houses a customs house, post office, and federal court. It has been restored to its 1861 appearance, when it hosted the Second Wheeling Convention that lead to West Virginia's independence from Virginia.

Oglebay Institute Mansion Museum: Park and museum with period rooms portraying the history of the Upper Ohio Valley; located in an imposing Greek Revival mansion. Adjacent is the *Oglebay Institute Glass Museum,* which contains the world famous five-foot-high Sweeney Punch Bowl, believed to be the largest piece of cut glass ever produced.

Eckhart House: Queen Anne Eclectic Victorian house, built in 1892. A beautifully decorated house that gives a good picture of Wheeling's history.

WEST VIRGINIA: THE SOUTH

Beckley

Beckley Exhibition Coal Mine: Mine operated in the late 1800s. Veteran coal miners take visitors on a tour of the mine in a "man trip" car.

Charleston

Capitol Complex: Designed by Cass Gilbert in 1932. The gold dome is the largest capitol dome in the United States; contains the *State Museum,* a craft shop, libraries, and a theater.

New River Gorge National River

One of the oldest rivers in the world, New River's white waters were troublesome to cross for Native Americans and early settlers until the *New River Gorge Bridge* was built in 1977—the longest single-arch steel span in the world and the second-highest bridge in the country—between the canyon rims on either side. *Hawk's Nest State Park* surrounds the river and offers amazing panoramic views.

VIRGINIA: THE NORTH

Alexandria

George Washington Masonic National Memorial: Situated on historic Shooters Hill, the awe-inspiring memorial overlooks the state capitol and houses the *George Washington Museum.* The tower also contains various elegantly decorated period rooms, a grand statue of Washington, and the beautiful *Knights Templar Chapel.*

Arlington

Pentagon: The headquarters of the United States Department of Defense, the Pentagon is one of the largest office buildings in the world. It houses 23,000 employees and stretches over 583 acres. Free tours are given daily.

Arlington National Cemetery: The graves of thousands of Americans represent every armed conflict the nation has seen. Memorials of special interest include the Tomb of the Unknown Soldier, the graves of John F. Kennedy and Jacqueline Kennedy Onassis, a Challenger Space Shuttle Memorial, a Confederate memorial, the graves of boxer Joe Louis and actor Lee Marvin, and many others. The cemetery also contains *Arlington House,* former home of the Confederate Civil War Gen. Robert E. Lee, which has been restored with period furnishings. Located within the cemetery is *Freedman's Village,* which was built for freed or refugee slaves after the outbreak of the Civil War. Their graves occupy their own section in the cemetery.

Charlottesville

Monticello Estate: Home of former President Thomas Jefferson, this stately mansion was designed by Jefferson himself over a period of 40 years and completed in 1809. It features 11,000 square feet of living space, and visitors can see 10 of the rooms and wander the extensive grounds.

Fredericksburg

Fredericksburg and Spotsylvania National Military Park: Four Civil War battles took place here, totaling 110,000 casualties, making it Virginia's bloodiest battleground. Also features the historic *"Stonewall" Jackson Shrine,* where the mythical war hero died; *Salem Church,* which was used as a hospital during the Civil War; and Civil War cemeteries.

Grottoes

Grand Caverns: Breathtaking scenery below the ground that easily matches the above-ground beauty of the surrounding Shenandoah Valley. Stalactites and stalagmites, draperies, and rare rock formations are only some of the features of these caverns, regarded to be the most impressive in the state.

Manassas

Manassas National Battlefield: The site of two major Civil War battles, in 1861 and 1862, though the main feature of the park is the imposing statue of Stonewall Jackson. More than 9,000 soldiers died here, and much of the landscape still bears the marks of the violent scenes. The railroad, which saw much of the fighting of the Battle of the Second Manassas (The Second Battle of Bull Run), has been left unfinished.

Mason Neck

Gunston Hall: Former home of George Mason, signer of the Declaration of Independence, this idyllic mansion and National Historic Landmark is a prime example of Georgian architecture.

Montpelier Station

Montpelier: Former home of James Madison, fourth president of the United States. Visitors can tour the elegant mansion, as well as the surrounding 200-acre forest, the restored formal gardens, the landscape arboretum, and the family and slave cemeteries.

Mount Vernon

Mount Vernon Estate and Gardens: The former home of George Washington has been restored to its 1799 appearance and is now the most visited historic home in the United States, after the White House. The founding father inhabited the mansion for 45 years and was himself the designer of the two-story piazza overlooking the Potomac River. Also at Mount Vernon is *George Washington's Gristmill,* today operated by costumed interpreters.

Strassburg

Crystal Caverns at Hupp's Hill: Probably the oldest documented cavern in the state, Crystal Caverns has unique rock formations. It is believed to have served as a refuge for runaway slaves, and historical tours are available with guides dressed in period costumes, who narrate the stories of Civil War soldiers by lantern light. In the same complex is also the *Stonewall Jackson Museum.*

Museum of American Presidents: Four of the United States's first five presidents, and a total of eight, were Virginians. This museum contains exhibits on their work and lives. Visitors can see letters handwritten by Thomas Jefferson and the desk at which the Constitution was written.

VIRGINIA: THE SOUTHWEST

Austinville
Shot Tower Historical State Park: The Shot Tower was built more than 150 years ago to produce ammunition for the early settlers. Molten lead from the Austinville Mines was dripped from the top of the tower to produce completely circular bullets. Visitors can ascend the tower.

Cumberland Gap National Historic Park
Visitors can tour *Hensley's Settlement,* which dates back to 1903, when the Hensleys decided to forsake civilization and become self-sufficient. This truly authentic and remote area has been fully restored, with 25 original buildings still remaining; *See also Middlesboro, East Tennessee.*

Hardy
Booker T. Washington National Monument: The tobacco plantation where the famous presidential advisor, orator, and educator shaped his ideas of education and race, and one of the few places where visitors can get an impression of the function of slavery on a small plantation.

Lynchburg
Point of Honor: The 18th-century home of Dr. George Cabell, Sr., is considered one of Virginia's most outstanding architectural achievements.

Natural Bridge
Natural Bridge: This unique rock formation has George Washington's initials carved into its side. Each night at dusk, visitors can watch the *Drama of Creation* lightshow by the bridge. The area contains various sites of interest, including nature walks to waterfalls and the *Saltpeter Cave,* which was used to produce gunpowder during the Civil War; the *Monacan Village,* a living history museum depicting the life of the Monacan Native Americans as they lived 300 years ago; *The Caverns,* the deepest caverns in the East; a *Wax Museum;* the world's largest exhibition of toys in the *Toy Museum;* and the *Monster Museum,* located in a "haunted" Victorian mansion.

Pocahontas
Historical Coal Mining Town: Virginia's first coal mining boom town, Pocahontas now features the world's first exhibition coal mine, with giant coal seams, and the Old Powerhouse—now a museum.

Roanoke
Explore Park: Environmental, historical, and recreational park; features three reconstructed historic areas depicting western Virginia life from 1000 AD to 1850. Actors in period costumes provide interpretative demonstrations of crafts, farm life, and Native American life.

VIRGINIA: THE SOUTHEAST

Appomattox
Appomattox Courthouse National Historical Park: Restored living history village, the park re-creates the closing days of the Civil War. Highlights include the surrender site of the McLean home and the village of Appomattox Court House, with 27 original 19th-century buildings.

Charles City
Berkeley Plantation: The most historic plantation in the state and the site of America's first Thanksgiving in 1619. The nation's first 10 presidents all spent time here, Lincoln reviewed his troops here, and it is the birthplace of Declaration of Independence signer Benjamin Harrison.

Fort Monroe
Fort Monroe: The largest stone fort in the United States, the fort is named after former President James Monroe and housed hundreds of escaped slaves during the Civil War. Today, the site is used as the headquarters of the Army's Training and Doctrine Command, but visitors can tour the fort and visit the **Casemate Museum.**

Gloucester
Rosewell Ruins: The ruins of one the finest mansions in Virginia, Rosewell has inspired poets and artists for centuries.

Norfolk
MacArthur Memorial: Imposing monument to the famous general, consisting of four separate buildings, including exhibition galleries; an education wing for students; and a museum with galleries that circle a monumental rotunda, the general's final resting place.
Battleship Wisconsin: Visitors experience the feel of being aboard an authentic U.S. battleship with missiles, 16-inch guns, and interior quarters.

Petersburg
Pamplin Historical Park & the National Museum of the Civil War Soldier: One of the finest Civil War museums in the United States, the park features an antebellum mansion, world-class museums, and a historic battlefield where Union soldiers seized the Confederate Capitol in April 1865.

Richmond
Hollywood Cemetery: Named after the holly trees that grow in the area, the cemetery has been made a Historical Landmark due to the many heroes of the Civil War that are buried here, including presidents James Monroe and John Tyler, several Civil War generals, and Confederate soldiers.
Museum and White House of Confederacy: Civil War museum considered one of the finest in America. Contains extensive collections on the period of the Confederacy, from military to political and domestic artifacts.
Museum of the Confederacy: Museum containing more than 15,000 Civil War and Confederacy artifacts.
Black History Museum & Cultural Center of Virginia: Celebrates the culture and history of African Americans from 1619 Jamestown until today. Features approximately 5,000 artifacts, documents, photographs, and pieces of art.

Virginia State Capitol: The first Classical revival building in the United States, dating from 1788. The rotunda contains a treasured life-sized statue of George Washington, the only one sculpted from life. The Old House of Delegates now houses a museum with collections of statuary, while the grounds outside feature the *Old Bell Tower* and statues of Virginia's heroes. Nearby is the *Old City Hall,* an impressive Victorian Gothic building built between 1886 and 1894, which occupies an entire city block.

Williamsburg
Colonial Williamsburg: America's largest living history site, featuring 88 original buildings, four museums, and hundreds of re-created houses, shops, workshops, and much more. Visitors can smell, watch, and hear the life of the 200-year-old colonial town bustling around them, and can eat and drink in re-created taverns.
Jamestown Settlement: Living history village reliving the events of 1607, when more than 100 English settlers arrived by boat in the New World and built America's first permanent English colony. The site features a historic film, a re-created colonial fort, boats, and a Powhatan village with hands-on demonstrations of how Native Americans and settlers lived at the time. Also on the site is *Yorktown Victory Center,* which takes visitors back to 1781 and re-creates the drama of the American Revolution. Visitors can enjoy a film and exhibitions inside, and outside they will find themselves in a Continental Army encampment or in an 18th-century farmhouse with interpreters introducing them to life in Virginia at the time.

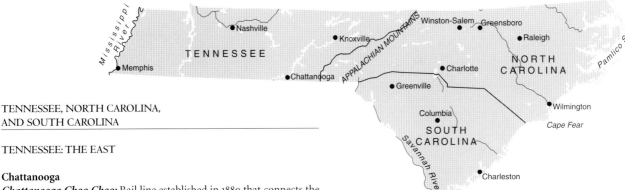

TENNESSEE, NORTH CAROLINA,
AND SOUTH CAROLINA

TENNESSEE: THE EAST

Chattanooga

Chattanooga Choo Choo: Rail line established in 1880 that connects the north and south part of town. The restored terminal features a restored engine, as well as shops and restaurants.

Chickamauga and Chattanooga National Military Park: The country's oldest Military Park, covering a large area in both Georgia and Tennessee. A series of important battles took place at Chattanooga in the fall of 1863. A visitor center at *Point Park* offers stunning views over the city.

Elizabethton

Sycamore Shoals State Historic Area: The site of the first permanent settlement outside colonial authority. The settlers encroached on Native American territory, the result being the Transylvania Purchase of more than 20 million acres of Native American land and the first written constitution by white settlers of American birth. The site has a museum and shows a film, and the frontier fort has been reconstructed. The site also contains the *John and Landon Carter Mansion*, a very interesting 1780s frame house.

Greeneville

Andrew Johnson National Historic Site: Commemorates the 17th president of the United States. The site contains a visitor center complex, which includes Johnson's tailor shop—his former trade—and his 1830s house. Also, the furnished *Homestead* where he lived from 1851 until his death is on the site, and the *Andrew Johnson National Cemetery* is at the edge of town.

Jonesborough

The oldest city in Tennessee and the capital of the state of Franklin for a short period from 1784. *Jonesborough Historic District* has more than 150 historic buildings in various styles.

Knoxville

Blount Mansion: The former home of territorial Gov. William Blunt. The mansion, built in 1792, became the center of political and social activity in the town. The grounds contain the *Governor's Office*, and the *Craighead Jackson House* features a visitor center and museum.

Limestone

Davy Crockett Birthplace State Park: A reproduced frontier cabin is the type of home Davy Crockett is likely to have lived in, and the site contains a large park and a monument to the hero.

Middlesboro

Cumberland Gap National Historic Park: The Gap forms a break in the Appalachian mountain chain and has a long history as the gateway to the western frontier. Between 1775 and 1810, 2-300,000 people crossed through here into unknown Kentucky.

Norris

Museum of Appalachia: An exceptional outdoor museum with more than 35 pioneer buildings. The cabins are furnished with such detail that the stories of the diverse people who once inhabited the buildings come to life, making visitors feel as if they have literally stepped back in time.

Pigeon Forge

Dollywood: Dolly Parton's colorful and crazy theme park, featuring rides, attractions, crafts, shows, concerts, and events.

Piney Flats

Rocky Mount: One of Tennessee's oldest houses. Features costumed interpreters, outbuildings, and a museum.

Rugby

Historic Rugby:
Founded in 1880 by Thomas Hughes as a cooperative community for younger sons of the English gentry, the restored Victorian town is now both an unspoiled living community and a historic site featuring 20 original buildings.

Vonore

Fort Loudoun State Historic Area: The site of one of the earliest British forts on the western frontier. Adjacent to the site is the *Sequoyah Birthplace Museum*, commemorating the famous Cherokee who developed a written language for his people.

CENTRAL TENNESSEE

Clarksville

Dunbar Cave: A 110-acre natural cave area of historical, natural, archaeological, and geological significance. Excavations show that the cave was occupied by humans for thousands of years.

Dover

Fort Donelson National Battlefield: The site of the first major Union victory in the Civil War, in February 1862, and where Gen. Ulysses S. Grant rose to fame. Original earthworks and an interpretive center are in the park.

Franklin

Carter House: Home of the Carter family, located just behind the site of the Battle of Franklin's heaviest fighting and now an interpretive center for the battle.

Lynchburg

Jack Daniel's Distillery: The oldest registered whiskey distillery in the country, founded in 1866. Guided tours are available, and the furnished 19th-century distillery office has been preserved.

Manchester

Old Stone Fort State Archaeological Park: Though the actual origins of the fort are unknown, it is believed that it was built by Indians of the Middle Woodland era in A.D. 430. The fort consists of walls and mounds that combine with cliffs and the river to form an enclosure.

Murfreesboro

Stones River National Battlefield: The site of a battle taking place around New Year 1863, after which Union forces took control of middle Tennessee. The site features parts of **Fortress Rosecrans,** with an interpretive museum, **Stones River National Cemetery**, and the **Hazen Brigade Monument**, believed to be the oldest Civil War monument.

Cannonsburgh: Complex of 20 historic buildings from the 19th and early 20th centuries, celebrating life in the rural South.

Nashville

Tennessee State Capitol: Completed in 1859 on a hill overlooking the city, the impressive Greek Revival structure stands as architect William Strickland's greatest achievement.

Tennessee State Museum: Featuring more than 70,000 square feet of exhibits, the museum interprets the history and culture of Tennessee.

Country Music Hall of Fame and Museum: The exterior of the building is shaped like a piano keyboard, and the museum covers more than 40,000 square feet and features a wall with every gold and platinum country music record that ever made the charts.

The Parthenon: The only full-scale replica of the ancient Greek temple in the world; houses the city's art collections and contains a famous sculpture of Athena by Alan LeQuire.

The Hermitage: Home of former President Andrew Jackson for more than 40 years. Originally erected in 1819, the Federal-style building was later rebuilt after a fire and is now furnished with original family pieces. The site also features a museum and a tomb.

Natchez Trace Parkway

Once the busiest trail in the South, the 400-mile trail through Mississippi to Middle Tennessee is now a parkway with markers pointing out historical sites on the way. Near **Howenwald** is the **Meriwether Lewis Monument,** marking the spot where the famous explorer was shot on October 11, 1809. A monument marks his grave in a nearby pioneer cemetery; *See also Natchez, Mississippi, for more sites along the trail.*

TENNESSEE: THE WEST

Memphis

Graceland: The biggest attraction in the state. Elvis Presley bought the house in 1957 at the age of 22, lived here for 20 years, and is buried in the garden. The house is furnished according to the rock star's both stylish and brash image, including the music room, the TV room with his record collection, and a hallway lined with gold and platinum records. The **Automobile Museum** features, among other things, Elvis's pink Cadillac.

Beale Street: Historical entertainment street, now one of America's most famous. Home to numerous concert venues and nightclubs, and the **Rock 'n' Soul Museum**, celebrating Memphis's musical history in its galleries.

Sun Studio: Known as the Birthplace of Rock 'n' Roll, it has housed stars like Roy Orbison, Jerry Lee Lewis, and Elvis Presley. Guided tours explain the history of the studio.

Pink Palace Museum and Planetarium: Named for its pink color, the palace serves as one of the largest museums in the Southeast and has exhibits on the cultural and natural history of Memphis.

National Civil Rights Museum: Housed in the Lorraine Motel, where Martin Luther King, Jr. was assassinated. By means of powerful and disturbing presentations, the museum interprets and informs on the Civil Rights Movement's impact on the wider context of worldwide human rights.

Pinson

Pinson Mounds State Archaeological Area: An important and unusual archaeological site dating mainly from A.D. 1-300 and featuring around 15 earthen mounds—the largest extant Middle Woodland mound group in the country—as well as a geometric enclosure, habitation areas, and related earthworks. The museum has a large collection of archaeological artifacts.

Shiloh

Shiloh National Military Park: The site of the first major, as well as the bloodiest, battle in the western theater of the Civil War. The park also contains the **Shiloh National Cemetery** and preserved prehistoric Indian mounds.

NORTH CAROLINA: THE COAST

Atlantic Beach

Fort Macon State Park: Has nature trails, a beach, a picnic area, and, most importantly, **Fort Macon Ramparts**, one of the finest examples of U.S. coastal forts. It was bombarded by Union troops during the Civil War and served as a defense base during World War II.

Kure Beach

Fort Fisher State Historic Site: During the Civil War, Fort Fisher was the last to fall to Union forces. The earthworks that are left are the largest in the South, and a battery has been restored and palisades re-created. The museum features a newly restored exhibit hall, and there is a visitor center and an audiovisual room. The **Fort Fisher-Southport Ferry** leaves from nearby and offers excellent views of Federal Point, Zeke's Island, the Rocks, and Price's Creek Lighthouse.

New Bern

Tryon Palace: Built in the 1760s and reconstructed in 1798, the mansion contains exquisite period furnishings and the complex features impressive gardens, costumed guides, and two smaller late 18th- and early 19th-century houses.

Southport

Old Brunswick Town State Historic Site: The first permanent European settlement was founded here in 1726. The town was involved in resistance to the Stamp Act, and was burt by the British in 1776. **Fort Anderson** was built on the site in 1862, the earthworks of which can still be seen.

Spruce Pine

Kings Mountain National Military Park: Contains the **Overmountain Victory National Historic Trail**, following the Revolutionary War route of Patriot soldiers to the Battle of Kings Mountain.

Stanfield

Reed Goldmine State Historic Site: Site of the first gold find in the country, it was a prosperous mine between 1803 and 1824. Today, visitors can explore part of the underground tunnels and see the original equipment in the museum.

Wilmington

Battleship North Carolina: Now a memorial to World War II veterans, the ship faced fierce combat in all major Pacific battles. Visitors can walk around nine decks and view the exhibits.

NORTH CAROLINA: THE OUTER BANKS

Cape Hatteras National Seashore

A protected seashore covering almost three islands, the shore off Hatteras Island is littered with salvage from the many shipwrecks in the area. *Cape Hatteras Lighthouse* is the most famous lighthouse on the Outer Banks and is the tallest in the nation. It is open to the public and has a visitor center with local history exhibits.

Kill Devil Hills

Wright Brothers National Memorial: The site of the first powered airplane flight, when Orville and Wilbur Wright made history; features a reconstruction of the brothers's camp, an airstrip and interpretive markers, a complete reproduction of their original plane, and a memorial stone.

Roanoke Island

Fort Raleigh National Historical Site: Although only a reconstructed earthen fort can be seen on the site, one of the most interesting parts of American history happened here. It was on this site that Sir Walter Raleigh unsuccessfully attempted to establish the so-called Lost Colony, and where Virginia Dare, the first English child in the New World, was born. The disappearance of the settlers in 1591 has sparked many a legend. Also on the site are the *Elizabethan Gardens,* illustrating the land the colonists had left and the one they had come to.

Roanoke Island Festival Park and Elizabeth II: One of the biggest attractions on the Outer Banks, the site serves as a history, educational, and cultural arts complex and has an array of activities to offer, including living history interpretations; an Adventure Museum, a Film Theater, concerts, an art gallery, etc. Also onsite is the reconstruction of the 1585 ship Elizabeth II.

NORTH CAROLINA: THE PIEDMONT

Bentonville Battleground State Historic Site

The largest battle of the Civil War fought in North Carolina took place on this site in February 1865, when Confederate Gen. Joseph E. Johnston attacked Gen. William T. Sherman's troops. More than 4,000 men were reported wounded, killed, or missing. Still on the site stands the *Harper House,* which was used as a field hospital, along with outdoor exhibits, monuments, the original earthworks and trenches, a Confederate cemetery, and a visitor center.

Burlington

Alamance Battleground State Historic Site: The site of a 1771 battle between a group of farmers, who called themselves Regulators in protest over abuse by government officials and the state militia under Gov. William Tryon. Also on the site is *Allen House,* a characteristic frontier log house.

Dallas

Town Creek Indian Mound: An elliptical mound, probably from the 16th-century Creek tribe. Also features a reconstructed village and an interpretive center.

Durham

Duke Homestead State Historic Site: The complex consists of the 1852 home and third tobacco factory of Washington Duke, a reconstruction of Duke's first factory, outbuildings, a packing house, and a curing barn.

Stagville Center: State Historic Site featuring 18th- and 19th-century buildings; focus on African American cultural history as exemplified by the still standing slave quarters of one of the largest plantations in the South.

Raleigh

North Carolina State Capitol: Greek Revival structure built in the 1830s. The capitol is in the shape of a Greek cross and has a copper-domed rotunda. On the lawn, 13 monuments and statues honor people and events of importance to the state.

Winston-Salem

Old Salem: One of the country's most outstanding examples of a preserved 18th-century community—91 of the original buildings, 15 of which are now museums.

NORTH CAROLINA: THE MOUNTAINS

Asheville

Biltmore Estate: One of the most opulent and elaborate buildings and the largest private residence in the United States. It was designed by Richard Morris Hunt in the style of a French Renaissance chateau, and the interior is decorated with all imaginable and unimaginable luxuries and artistry. The gardens were designed by Frederick Law Olmsted. Many of the original farm buildings are open to the public, and a model village in the Tudor style, the *Biltmore Estate Historic District,* ornaments the entrance to the estate.

Cherokee

Cherokee Indian Reservation: The largest American Indian reservation in the East. The *Museum of the Cherokee Indian* has the most comprehensive collection of Native American artifacts in the state. The *Oconaluftee Indian Village* is re-created as it was in the 1750s and features historical exhibitions, crafts demonstrations, and much more.

Weaverville

Vance Birthplace: Pioneer farmstead and birthplace of Zebulon B. Vance, Civil War officer, governor of North Carolina, and United States senator. The picturesque site includes the main log house and outbuildings, a cemetery, and a museum.

Wilkesboro

Old Wilkes Jail Museum: The jail was functioning from its completion in 1860 until the construction of a new prison in 1915. Once held Tom Dula (Tom Dooley).

SOUTH CAROLINA: NORTHWEST AND CENTRAL

Bishopville

South Carolina Cotton Museum: Interpretive history museum with exhibits on this lucrative industry of the South.

Brattonsville

Historic Brattonsville District: Includes the *Revolutionary War Battlefield Site,* commemorating the Battle of Huck's Defeat in 1780, one of the first victories over the British cavalry; a living history village and farm; historic buildings open to visitors; and wilderness trails.

Camden

The site of two major Revolutionary War battles: the Battle of Camden and the Battle of Hobkirk's Hill. *Historic Camden Park* is a 98-acre battle site containing a collection of relocated and reconstructed 18th- and 19th-century houses, including the *Kershaw House,* home of the city's founder and used by British Gen. Charles Cornwallis as his Revolutionary War headquarters.

Chesnee

Cowpens National Battlefield: Commemorates a decisive battle of the Revolution in January 1781. The field contains a restored 1830s cabin and a visitor center with weapons exhibits.

Columbia

South Carolina Governor's Mansion: Built in 1855, the mansion has been home to the state's governors since 1868. The building's public rooms hold rich treasures of silver, porcelain, furniture, paintings, and documents that illustrate the culture and history of the state.

South Carolina State House: At almost 150 years old, this impressive Italian Renaissance Revival building houses a large portrait gallery, and on the exterior, bronze stars mark the spots hit by General Sherman's troops when he ordered them to fire on February 16, 1865.

South Carolina State Museum: Housed in the 1895 cotton-producing *Columbia Duck Mill,* the museum follows the history of the state's art, natural, science and technology, and cultural history.

Francis Marion National Forest

Swampland named after a Revolutionary War hero who conducted guerilla warfare and escaped British forces by disappearing into the swamps. The area contains the prehistoric *Sewee Shell Ring*, and an interpretive trail takes visitors past the ring and offers views of the salt marsh.

Kings Mountain National Military Park
The park includes the site of one of the worst battles of the American Revolution, the Battle of Kings Mountain on October 7, 1780. The visitor center features a film, diorama, and exhibitions on the battle. Adjacent is the **Kings Mountain State Park**, which has a living history museum demonstrating life in the mid-19th century.

Ninety Six
Ninety Six National Historic Site: Contains the original ruins of the 17th-century town and fort, which was the site of the South's first Revolutionary War battle in 1775 and of the Continental army's longest siege during the Revolution. A visitor center has exhibits and information.

Spartanburg
Walnut Grove Plantation: An early plantation house built around 1765, with period furnishings. The complex includes various outbuildings, among them a 1777 kitchen, smokehouse, barn, well house, the first school in the area, and a doctor's office.

SOUTH CAROLINA: THE COAST

Charleston and surrounds
Old Exchange and Provost Dungeon: One of the most historically significant buildings in the nation, having witnessed imprisoned pirates, colonels, and politicians, the declaration of the state's independence from the colonial power, and a ball held for George Washington.

Charleston Museum: America's first museum, founded in 1773. Extensive exhibits examine the history of the Low Country, and the museum also possesses several historic houses—most notably the *Heyward-Washington House,* dating from 1772, with its impressive woodwork and magnificent collection of locally made furniture.

Drayton Hall: Completed in 1742, it is the oldest preserved plantation house in the country that is open to visitors. One of the finest examples of Georgian-Palladian architecture, it stands nearly untouched. The focus here is architectural detail, as the house has been left unfurnished.

Magnolia Plantation and Gardens: The ancestral home of the Drayton family for three centuries, featuring one of the most stunning gardens in the world. The plantation also includes a range of other attractions, such as a petting zoo, specialized gardens, arts and antique galleries, a slave cabin, and the *Audubon Swamp Garden* with its wild birds and reptiles.

Mt. Pleasant
Boone Hall Plantation: Though the present house was built in 1935, after the original plantation house fell into ruin, the original slave cabins and other outbuildings are still on the grounds. The plantation is still a working estate but is open for visitors.

St. Helena Island
Penn Center: The country's first school for freed slaves and one of the most important sites in African-American history. The district comprises 19 buildings, among them the *Brick Church*, burial grounds, *Gantt Cottage*, the lodgings of Martin Luther King, Jr., and large nature areas.

Sullivan's Island
Fort Sumter: Designed for the defense of Charleston Harbor, construction started in 1827 on the man-made Sullivan's Island. The fort received the opening shots of the Civil War in April 1861.

Fort Multrie: The site has seen more than 170 years of coastal defense, though the present fort dates from 1809.

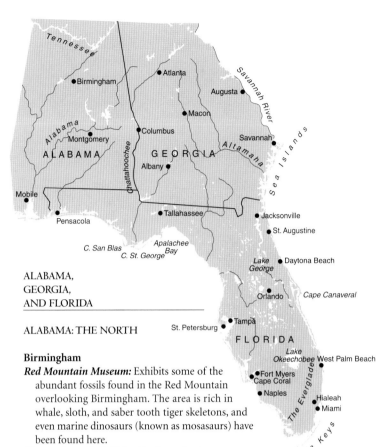

ALABAMA,
GEORGIA,
AND FLORIDA

ALABAMA: THE NORTH

Birmingham
Red Mountain Museum: Exhibits some of the abundant fossils found in the Red Mountain overlooking Birmingham. The area is rich in whale, sloth, and saber tooth tiger skeletons, and even marine dinosaurs (known as mosasaurs) have been found here.

Birmingham Civil Rights Institute: Looks at the important development of civil rights in the United States and offers a personalized look at the individuals of the 1950s and 1960s who braved the order of the day for the sake of combating bigotry and racial discrimination.

Alabama Jazz Hall of Fame: Honors the accomplishments of great jazz artists with ties to Alabama—including Nat King Cole, Duke Ellington, and Erskine Hawkins.

Bridgeport
Russell Cave National Monument: Cave shelter with archaeological records of more than 9,000 years of occupation; includes living history demonstrations, hiking trails passing archaeological excavations, and a visitor center with prehistoric artifacts.

Cullman
Clarkson Covered Bridge: A typical example of Alabama's many covered wooden bridges, this is the longest, at 296 feet, and doubles as the site of the Battle of Hog Mountain in April 1863.

Hanceville
The Shrine at Our Lady of the Angels Monastery: With their truly beautiful and awe-inspiring architecture amid the green rolling hills of Alabama, this church is worth a visit for both tourists and those seeking spiritual rest.

Huntsville
Alabama Constitution Village: A living history museum consisting of four rebuilt main buildings with outbuildings; dates from the beginning of the 19th century, when the 1819 Constitutional Convention was written.

U.S. Space and Rocket Center: With a multitude of different exhibits, the space center offers the largest hands-on space experience in the world, including NASA guided tours, Omnimax films, an unparalleled museum collection, a full-scale space shuttle exhibit, and space simulators.

McCalla

Tannehill Ironworks State Park: Some of the first iron-processing facilities in the state are still kept here, along with refurnished pioneer cabins, a country store, a gristmill, and a museum.

CENTRAL ALABAMA

Cahaba

Old Cahaba Archaeological Park: A ghost town until recently, Cahaba's rehabilitation as an archaeological complex includes reconstructed streets and ruins with interpretive signs, an 1840s wood-framed house, a welcome center, a picnic area, and hiking trails.

Daviston

Horseshoe Bend National Military Park: The site of the final battle of the Creek War in 1814, the park now features exhibitions on Creek culture and a marked tour of the battle.

Demopolis

Gaineswood: Between 1842 and 1860, this now impressive mansion went through an incredible transformation from a plain log house to a regency villa. It is one of the most interesting houses in the country and is particularly notable for its imposing architecture and its Greek Revival interior.

Montevallo

The American Village: A re-creation of a colonial village. The Village Green features Washington Hall, the Colonial Courthouse, and the President's Oval Office.

Montgomery

Alabama State Capitol: Despite various remodelings between its original construction in 1847 and its now Neoclassical appearance, the capitol still looks harmoniously proportioned, while at once reflecting 140 years of changing fashions in architecture and furnishings. A bronze star on the portico marks the spot of Jefferson Davis's inauguration.

First White House of the Confederacy: Modest Italianate house, in which Confederate President Jefferson Davis lived while Montgomery was the capital of the Confederacy.

Old Alabama Town: The 40 buildings of this village reflect various social classes—from a doctor's office and a town house to a blacksmith shop and a one-room schoolhouse.

Tuscaloosa

University of Alabama: The university comprises some of the most interesting architecture in the city, for instance **Gorgas House**, dating from 1829, which was designed by William Nichols and has a fine collection of silver, decorative arts, and furniture. Also on campus are the impressive Greek Revival **President's Mansion**, the paradoxically octagonal **Little Round House**, and the **Old Observatory**, the only classroom that survived an attack by the Unionists.

Moundville Archaeological Park: The site of a prehistoric city, the park spans 320 acres and has 20 mounds, probably built by ancestors of the Choctaw. The city boasted 3,000 inhabitants during its heyday in the 12th and 13th centuries. A museum exhibits archeological findings, including skeletons.

Tuskegee

Tuskegee Institute National Historic Site: Booker T. Washington pioneered the history of education when he founded the Tuskegee Institute in 1881, the first trade school for black students. The school comprises around 160 buildings, built with student-made bricks and raised with student labor. **The Oaks**, Washington's home, still contains the original furniture. The **George Washington Carver Museum** honors Dr. Carver's ingenious contributions to the school in the areas of horticulture and chemistry and contains his instruments and his plant collections.

Wetumpka

Fort Toulouse and Jackson Park: Two forts have been re-created at this spot: Fort Toulouse, built by French explorer Bienville in 1717; and Fort Jackson, built by Andrew Jackson during his war against the local Creeks. There is a museum with archeological findings and costumed tours.

ALABAMA: THE GULF COAST AND SOUTHEAST

Mobile

Fort Condé: This partially reconstructed 18th-century fort re-creates its days as the capitol of the Louisiana Territory. The fort houses a museum, and the furnished quarters feature staff dressed in French colonial uniforms. The fort also houses the city's ***visitor center***.

Oakleigh: The official antebellum home of Mobile, this beautiful Greek Revival mansion, built during the 1830s, houses exquisite period collections of furniture, silver, porcelain, and toys.

Battleship USS **Alabama:** In this 100-acre memorial park, the refurbished World War II battleship USS *Alabama* is open for inspection, along with the submarine USS *Drum*, the B-52 *Stratofortress*, and the A-12 *Blackbird* spy plane.

Bellingrath Gardens and Home: This beautiful house has a fine collection of china and porcelain, but its real attraction lies in the 800-acre park—of which 65 acres are the ever-blooming Bellingrath Gardens.

Mobile Bay

Fort Gaines: Guards the entrance to Mobile Bay, which is supported on the other side by **Fort Morgan**. Both forts house museums, but Fort Morgan is the better preserved of the two. The star-shaped fort endured a two-week siege during the Civil War, which is documented in the museum's numerous military artifacts.

Historic Blakeley Park: The park—the largest National Historic Register Site east of the Mississippi—contains preserved breastworks, rifle pits, and redoubts from the 1865 Union attack, as well as middens and mounds from habitation spanning 4,000 years. The site also contains the beautiful 1814 ghost town, the City of Blakeley.

Audubon Bird Sanctuary: Situated on Dauphin Island, it has been rated one of the best birding locations in the country. The sanctuary comprises beaches, swamp, hardwood forest, dunes, and a freshwater lake; trails throughout the area.

Ozark

Army Aviation Museum: This museum houses the world's largest collection of helicopters, along with other army aircraft.

Claybank Church: Constructed from coarse logs, this historic 1852 church has a very rough and rustic expression that reflects the atmosphere of the historic South.

Troy

Pike Pioneer Museum: This little museum village is comprised of more than a century old log houses, tenant houses, a general store, and 15 acres of wooded land. The museum also has craft demonstrations and exhibitions of furniture, clothing, and carriages.

GEORGIA: THE NORTH

Atlanta

Georgia State Capitol: Built in 1889 and designed by Edbrooke & Burnham, the capitol building carries a beautiful gilded dome surmounted by a statue of liberty.

Atlanta History Center and Museum: The vast museum narrates Atlanta's history from Native American settlement to colonization, cotton growing, and the Civil War. The History Center also includes historic houses, a research library, and 32 acres of gardens.

High Museum of Art: Architect Richard Meier designed the spectacular award-winning building that houses the museum. The museum is one of the best in the Southeast, and its fine collections include 19th-century American paintings, sculptures, and decorative arts.

Martin Luther King, Jr. National Historic Site: A stretch of 10 blocks with markers on a number of the buildings that were of importance to the development of the black community in Atlanta.

Cartersville
Etowah Indian Mounds: The mounds and artifacts found in this city, which once held several thousand people, date from 1,000 to 1,500 and document the Etowah's extensive travels.

Fort Oglethorpe
Chickamauga and Chattanooga National Military Park: The nation's first military park, Chickamauga Battlefield was the site of one of the bloodiest battles of the Civil War on September 19–20, 1863. The events of the battle can be followed on a tour road with markers and monuments, and the visitor center has a weapons collection.

Macon
Ocmulgee National Monument: The site of continued occupation for 10,000 years. An unusual number of excavated artifacts are on display, as well as mounds built between AD 900 and 1100 and a reconstructed earth lodge.

Stone Mountain Park
Stone Mountain, the largest piece of exposed granite in the world, has been the meeting place for Native American tribes and early settlers for centuries. In amazing relief in the rock are the carved figures of Confederate President Jefferson Davis, Gen. Robert E. Lee, and Gen. Stonewall Jackson. Contained in the 3,200-acre park is also the **Memorial Hall Museum**, exhibiting Civil War paraphernalia and a complex of 19 antebellum structures.

Washington
A treasure of historic homes, Washington's streets are lined with beautiful Greek Revival structures, one of the earliest dating back to 1794. **Callaway Plantation** is now a living history museum and a working plantation, with a wide range of authentic furnished buildings.

GEORGIA: THE SOUTHWEST

Andersonville
Andersonville National Historic Site: The Civil War's most notorious prisoner-of-war camp held up to 32,000 prisoners. The 13,000 prisoners who died there are buried at the **Andersonville National Cemetery**. There is a small museum and visitor center.

Columbus
Coca-Cola Space Science Center: Opened in 1996, the space center provides unique hands-on experience. The center includes a planetarium, the Challenger Learning Center, and exhibit areas.

Lumpkin
Providence Canyon: Georgia's "Little Grand Canyon" is famed for its rare wild flowers and its beautiful scenery.

Plains
Jimmy Carter National Historic Site: The site commemorates the former president including his boyhood home and later home, his school, and visitor center.

Tifton
Agrirama: Living history museum with 18th- to early 20th-century farm buildings and equipment, including a church, gristmill, blacksmith shop, sawmill, tram, etc.

GEORGIA: THE COAST

Jekyll Island
Jekyll Island Club Historic District: The Jekyll Island Club was established in 1886 and was seen as one of the most exclusive clubs in the United States. With a maximum of 100 members, they had luxurious "cottages" and a club house, which visitors can tour.

Okefenokee Swamp
Vast and mysterious wilderness with a variety of wildlife, including alligators, snakes, and cranes, this 700-square-mile swamp is the largest peat-producing bog swamp in the nation. The swamp can be toured from four parks, and sightseeing, boating, and fishing are popular activities.

Savannah
Old Fort Jackson: One of the city's most popular tourist attractions, the old fort has played a pivotal role in defending Savannah since the beginning of the 18th century. Visitors can tour the fort—the oldest in Georgia—and there is a museum with military paraphernalia.

Fort Pulaski National Monument: Reconstructed old fort, which was captured by Union Major Gen. David Hunter in April 1862. The park includes more than 5,000 acres of marsh and uplands.

Savannah History Museum: Situated on the site of an unsuccessful siege by American and French troops in 1779, the museum is housed in the 1860 Georgia Railroad depot. Multimedia presentations and information on the National Historic Landmark District, where the 17-site **African-American Trail Tour** also begins, are available.

St. Simons Island
Fort Frederica National Monument: Founded in 1736 by Georgia founder James Edward Oglethorpe to protect the area against the Spanish, this historic fort once encompassed a whole town. Only a few buildings are still left inside the fort. There are exhibitions on local history and the town, and interpreters in period costumes demonstrating crafts in the summer.

Tybee Island
Tybee Island Lighthouse and Museum: One of the most intact historical lighthouses in the United States, Tybee Island Lighthouse still has all its buildings dating back to 1732. Visitors can ascend the 178 steps to the top and visit the museum.

FLORIDA: THE NORTH

Fernandina Beach
Fort Clinch State Park: Civil War fort constructed in the 1840s. The park includes extensive wildlife habitats and recreational facilities.

Jacksonville
Fort Caroline National Memorial: Early French colony, built in 1564 by French Huguenots and Timucuans. The Spanish captured the fort in 1565. The present site contains a reconstruction of the fort and a museum and visitor center.

Pensacola
Fort Pickens: Impressive old fort, built in the 1830s by Americans to defend the naval shipyard in Pensacola. Apache Chief Geronimo was imprisoned here 1886–8.

Pensacola Naval Air Station: Constructed in 1914, the first naval aviation training base in the country is now home to the Blue Angels flying squadron and contains the **National Museum of Naval Aviation**; the restored Civil War **Fort Barrancas**; and the 1797 **Bateria de San Antonio**.

St. Augustine
Castillo de San Marcos National Monument: An impressive historic fort,

this large structure was built 1672–1756 and is the oldest in the city. Its 12-foot-thick walls withstood major sieges in 1702 and 1740, and today the fort stands much as it did three centuries ago.

Fountain of Youth: Archaeological park containing St. Augustine's first mission and colony. Visitors can drink from the spring claimed to be the Fountain of Youth, which was discovered by Spanish explorer Ponce de Leon. The park also contains one of the most important Indian burial grounds in the Southeast, as well as the Timucua Indian Exhibit.

Tallahassee

Museum of Florida History: Consists of five different sites. The main museum exhibits artifacts, reproductions, graphics, and hands-on materials that examine Florida's history from the Pleistocene period to the present. Also managed by the museum is the *Old State Capitol.* Built in 1845 when Florida was admitted to the Union, the interior of the Old Capitol has been restored and now houses a museum that contains, among other things, the original Florida Constitution and artifacts from the Colonial period and the Seminole War. *Mission San Luis de Apalachee* was the capital of the Spanish missions, 1656–1704, and boasted a population of 1,400 Apalachee. The village is now being developed into a living history park with a reconstruction of a 17th-century mission. *Union Bank* is the state's oldest bank, dating back to 1841, and now also serves as a museum, as does the beautifully restored *Knott House Museum.*

CENTRAL FLORIDA

Bradenton

De Soto National Memorial: Situated on what may have been the spot where explorer Hernando de Soto landed in 1539, the memorial commemorates his journey through North America. The site features costumed interpreters and musket firing. Nearby is the *Fort de Soto Park,* a nature sanctuary containing the fort built in 1898 to defend Tampa Bay.

Crystal River

Crystal River State Archaeological Site: This important pre-Columbian site contains burial mounds, a temple, and a large plaza. The museum displays archaeological finds from the site.

Dade City

Pioneer Florida Museum and Village: The museum commemorates the simple values of the pioneers, their craftsmanship, and their everyday life and work. Also contained in the grounds are a small, relocated schoolhouse, a church, the Trilby depot, and a train engine.

Orlando

Walt Disney World: One of the world's biggest holiday attractions, Disney World features four major theme parks, as well as a multitude of rides, exhibitions, shows, restaurants, etc.

John F. Kennedy Space Center: Where the first U.S. space satellite was sent off in 1958, the first Americans sent into space in 1961, and where *Apollo 11* set off for the moon in 1969. The *NASA Space Center Visitor Center* displays rockets, engines, and recovered capsules, while a bus tour takes visitors around the complex where they are also given the chance to experience a simulation of the *Apòllo 11* takeoff.

Orlando Science Center: A large hands-on center with hundreds of interactive opportunities, films, and exhibitions.

Sarasota

John & Mable Ringling Museum of Art: Collected by circus magnate John Ringling, the country's largest museum complex houses a fine and flamboyant art collection, as well as Ringling's elaborate mansion *Ca' d'Zan,* built to resemble the Doge's Palace in Venice.

St. Petersburg

Salvador Dali Museum: Art museum containing the world's largest collection of paintings by the famous Spanish surrealist.

FLORIDA: THE SOUTH

Everglades National Park

The only subtropical reserve in North America, the Everglades have a unique flora and fauna. Boating, canoeing, hiking, and fishing can be done in the park, and some of the five visitor centers have interpretive resources. At the *Miccosukee Indian Village,* visitors can experience the Miccosukee people's way of life, their culture, and their history. And the *Big Cypress Reservation* of the Seminole tribe contains a museum, activities, and campgrounds.

Fort Myers

Edison Winter Home: Built in 1886, the house and laboratory are still almost as Edison left them. The house is surrounded by the lush tropical garden he used for rubber experiments, and the museum includes 170 phonographs. The adjacent *Henry Ford Winter Home* is still furnished in the style of the 1920s.

Key West

Key West Historic District: Encompassing some 3,100 buildings, the varied architecture of the district tells the history of Key West.

Ernest Hemingway House: The house in which the famous author lived, on and off from 1931 until his death in 1961. The house contains a bookstore and is inhabited by 60 cats.

Dry Tortugas National Park: Consists of seven isolated islands west of Key West and is famous for its bird and marine life, as well as for its legends of pirates and sunken treasures. *Fort Jefferson,* the United States's largest 19th-century coastal fort, dominates the park.

Miami

Known as the home of Art Deco, more than 800 private and commercial buildings are still preserved in Miami's *Art Deco Historic District. Coral Gables* is a Moorish-Spanish planned community, while *Opa-locka* has Moorish-style buildings and patterned streets.

Vizcaya Museum and Gardens: The grandest house in the state, Villa Vizcaya is an elaborate example of the Mediterranean Revival Style. Decorated with rare antiquities and decorative arts, and with a large formal garden of mixed Italian and local design.

Holocaust Memorial: Honors the six million Jews killed during World War II, with an impressive and very powerful sculpture in the shape of a hand rising from the ground with people climbing up the arm.

Palm Beach

A resort and seasonal home for the wealthy, Palm Beach is dominated by imposing mansions, one the most impressive being Henry Morrison Flagler's *Whitehall.* The image of opulence down to the minutest detail, the mansion is now the *Henry Morrison Flagler Museum* and contains Flagler's furnishings and memorabilia, as well as collections of early 20th century art and clothing.

ARKANSAS, LOUISIANA, AND MISSISSIPPI

ARKANSAS: THE NORTHWEST AND THE OZARKS

Bull Shoals
Mountain Village 1890: Historic re-creation of a pioneer village containing 11 authentic main buildings, including a bank, jail, blacksmith shop, and sawmill. Nearby are the ***Bull Shoals Caverns***, which were formed 350 million years ago.

Cotter
Cotter Bridge: Rainbow-arched bridge, built in 1930 and ranked among the most beautiful sights in mid-America.

Eureka Springs
Abundant Memories Heritage Village: Historic village in mountain setting; features 25 buildings, Civil and Revolutionary War collections, a blacksmith shop, wagons, an apothecary, and other artifacts and reconstructions, as well as a historama show enacted on five stages.
Elna N. Smith Foundation Site: Site with a Christian theme and various religious and educational attractions, such as the seven-story statue ***Christ of the Ozarks;*** *The New Holy Land* historic exhibit with costumed guides that take visitors through the history and culture of the ancient Middle East; several village churches; a ten-foot section of the Berlin Wall; and ***The Great Passion Play*** shown all summer.
Rosalie House: Victorian house built in the 1880s, displaying the splendor of upper-class Victorian life.

Flippin
White River Scenic Railroad: Visitors can experience a several-hour ride along the White River in an original steam train still featuring the old passenger seats.

Fort Smith
Fort Smith National Historic Site: Features the remains of two frontier forts and the Federal Court for the Western District of Arkansas. The visitor center examines the history of the area, and visitors can also see "Hangin' Judge" Isaac C. Parker's courtroom and reproductions of the gallows and jail.

Jacksonport State Park
A steamboat port and an occupied town during the Civil War, the state park now features the restored 1869 courthouse with exhibits, and the Mary Woods II, a reconstructed 1880s steamboat.

Mountain View
Ozark Folk Center State Park: Historic pioneer village that works to preserve the traditional Ozark way of life. Pioneer skills and crafts are demonstrated, and visitors can learn to play the dulcimer, dance, or grow an herb garden.

Pea Ridge
Pea Ridge National Military Park: A well-preserved Civil War battlefield commemorating the May 1863 battle, after which Missouri remained under Union control. The site includes the reconstructed wartime structure Elkhorn Tavern.

Prairie Grove
Prairie Grove Battlefield State Park: Includes buildings depicting Civil War–era life in the area, and a museum examining the effect of the Civil War on the people of the Ozarks.

CENTRAL ARKANSAS

Hot Springs
Hot Springs National Park: The oldest national park in America; contains 47 hot springs that fed the famous resort and gave rise to the picturesque ***Bathhouse Row***, which consists of eight spa bathhouses dating from 1911 to 1935. There is also a visitor center and a museum.

Little Rock
Old State House Museum: 1836 Greek revival building and the oldest state capitol west of the Mississippi. A multimedia museum focuses on state history, especially women's history and political history.
Historic Arkansas Museum: Tours can be made of five 19th-century houses, with costumed actors and changing exhibits. The museum building houses the state collection of paintings, furniture, pottery, silver, textiles, and firearms.

Toltec Mounds Archaeological State Park
One of the largest and most complex groups of ancient earthworks in the Lower Mississippi Valley, occupied from approximately A.D. 700 to 950.

ARKANSAS: THE SOUTH AND EAST

Gillet
Arkansas Post National Memorial: A memorial and a museum mark the site of a trading post established by Henri de Tonti in 1686 and believed to be the first semipermanent European settlement in the lower Mississippi River Valley.

Jonesboro
Arkansas State University Museum: Exhibitions include galleries on Native American, natural and military history, Arkansas archaeology, and the Old Town Arkansas Exhibit (which features turn-of-the-century shops and buildings).

Louisiana Purchase State Park
The site where all surveys for the Louisiana Purchase were determined in 1815. A marked boardwalk leads to a monument marking the site, which lies in the swamp.

Murfreesboro
Crater of Diamonds State Park: The only diamond-bearing site that is open to the public. Visitors can search for gem stones and keep anything they find for themselves.

Old Washington Historic State Park
Preserved 19th-century town containing the Confederate Capitol, the 1874 courthouse (now the visitor center), antebellum houses, the Tavern Inn, a blacksmith shop, and a weapons museum.

Parkin Archeological State Park
The best-preserved site from A.D. 1000 to around 1550 in the area; believed to have been the Native American village of Casqui, which Hernando de Soto visited in 1541. Contains a large ceremonial mound, a museum, and an interpretive center.

Rison
Pioneer Village: Re-creation of a 19th-century pioneer village with craft shops, store, and log cabins.

LOUISIANA: THE NORTH AND EAST

Audubon State Historic Site
This park celebrates the 1820s New Orleans artist John James Audubon, who was particularly famous for his bird paintings.

Baton Rouge
Lafayette Buildings: Examples of the French character of the town, these 1760s houses have cast-iron galleries reminiscent of the French Quarter in New Orleans.

Old State Capitol: This 1849 building sports a large spiral iron staircase reaching toward the stained-glass rotunda above. In 1861, Louisiana voted to secede from the Union in this building.

Louisiana State Capitol: The new capitol takes the form of a 34-story skyscraper with a panoramic view and was built in 1932 by U.S. senator-to-be Huey P. Long, who was later assassinated in the same building.

Pentagon Barracks: Construction started in 1819 by soldiers, and the four remaining buildings stand on the site of an 18th-century British fort. Apart from the lieutenant governor's office and apartments for legislators, the barracks also contain the **Capitol Complex Visitor Center.**

Old Arsenal: The military post, which was discontinued in 1879, hides behind a 10-foot-high brick wall and was temporarily the site of Louisiana State University. It also serves as a burial ground for Union soldiers, contains a Native American ceremonial mound, and has two cannon commemorating the 1779 Battle of Baton Rouge.

Louisiana Arts and Science Center: Has a historic house, the **Old Governor's Mansion**, which has been furnished to illustrate the styles of the times of the nine governors that lived there.

Beauregard Town: Laid out in the style of a European town from 1806.

Magnolia Mound: This French-West Indian house from the 1790s is in a magnolia grove and was occupied by indigo planter John Joyce. It was later updated in the Federal style in which it appears today, and it now houses collections of English silver, French porcelain, and Philadelphia and New York furniture.

Epps
Poverty Point State Historic Site: One of the most important archaeological sites, these earthworks from a prehistoric Native American village, built between 1700 and 1100 B.C., show evidence of what could be the earliest culture found in the Mississippi Valley. The site contains earthen mounds and evidence of trade, the *Poverty Point National Monument*—the largest prehistoric earthworks in North America—as well as an interpretive museum and guided tours.

Garyville
San Francisco: A magnificent mid-19th-century house in the uncommon (for Louisiana) "Steamboat Gothic" style, with extravagant decoration of both the exterior and interior.

Marksville
Marksville State Historic Site: Contains archaeological evidence of Native Americans from A.D. 100 to 400, apparently related to the Hopewell culture in Ohio. Visitors can see a group of burial mounds as well as archaeological finds in the **museum.**

Monroe
Watson Brake Earthen Mound Complex: Believed to be the oldest mound site in the country, the 11 mounds date back to 3400-1800 B.C. The mounds are connected by ridges to form an oval approximately 850 feet across.

Natchitoches
Fort Jean Baptiste: Built by the French in 1715, the original wooden fort was later taken over by the Spanish and used as a trading center. The present construction is a replica.

St. Francisville
Rosedown: Finished in 1838, this is one of the finest plantation houses in the state, exhibiting exquisite craftsmanship and designs taken from the resident couple's travels in Europe. The gardens sport an alley of 200-year-old oaks and many colorful flowers.

Zachary
Port Hudson State Historic Site: An area of strategic importance, it was fortified in 1862 when Union troops occupied New Orleans. In 1863, Gen. Franklin Gardner led one of the bloodiest battles of the war at Fort Desperate but was forced to surrender in July 1863. The area features a museum, and a trail and boardwalks lead visitors to breastworks on the battlefield and the viewing tower at Fort Desperate.

LOUISIANA: NEW ORLEANS AND BAYOU COUNTRY

Lafayette
Vermilionville: Living history museum recreating Cajun and Creole life and featuring period homes.

Acadian Village: Folk life museum consisting mostly of authentic 19th-century furnished buildings, including simple cypress cottages, a chapel, village store, sheds, and barns.

New Iberia
Conrad Rice Mill: In operation since 1912, this may be the oldest operating rice mill in the country; slide show and tour available.

New Orleans: French Quarter or Vieux Carré
First successful settlement established by French explorer Bienville in 1718. His landing spot, **Jackson Square**, is flanked by magnificent colonial buildings and the **Saint Louis Cathedral**, which was rebuilt various times between 1722 and 1851. Other historic buildings include the **Hermann-Grima House**; the **Ursuline Convent**, which is possibly the oldest European building in the Mississippi River valley; and the **Beauregard-Keyes House,** once inhabited by Confederate Gen. Pierre T. Beauregard and later by author Frances Parkinson Keyes.

French Market: Historic 1790's marketplace on the Mississippi.

Old U.S. Mint: Produced coins from as early as 25 years before the Civil War and again from 1879 to 1909. An impressive building, its vaulted interior now serves as an exhibition space.

Historic New Orleans Collection: Temporary and permanent exhibitions; contains an 1889 townhouse decorated in early 20th-century style.

Mardi Gras: Seasonal parade and carnival celebrated worldwide, though it is nowhere near as colorful as in New Orleans.

New Orleans: Garden District
Built by the most successful and socially ambitious Americans after the Louisiana Purchase in 1803, this area of the city is characterized by classic antebellum houses with colonnades and expansive gardens. Classic examples include the Greek Revival **Strachan House,** from 1850, and the **Maddox-Brennan House,** with its cast-iron gate and elaborate doorway. In remembrance of the original Garden District inhabitants, the elaborate tombs of the 1833 **Lafayette Cemetery Number 1** contrast with the rows of vaults of the less affluent citizens of New Orleans.

Outer New Orleans
Jean Lafitte National Historical Park and Preserve: Six separate sites that highlight different features of Louisiana culture and natural resources, one of which is the site of the Battle of New Orleans, the final battle of the War of 1812. The battlefield, the Chalmette section of the park, contains **Chalmette National Cemetery** and **Beauregard House,** designed by James Gallier, Sr., as well as a **visitor center** with exhibits on the battle and details of the war. The park also contains the **Chitamacha Cultural Center**, which displays the craft work of the Chitamachas.

Thibodaux

Laurel Valley Village Museum: Formerly a large sugar plantation, Laurel Valley is a rare example of an original, intact plantation. It contains a complex of 1840s structures, such as a manor house, barns, slave cabins, a smithy, schoolhouse, general store, and ruins of the sugar mill.

Washington

Arlington House: Built in 1829 for Amos Webb, the house is one of the largest plantation houses in the country and today serves as a memorial to Gen. Robert E. Lee, who lived in the house for 30 years.

MISSISSIPPI: THE NORTH

Columbus

Waverley Plantation: This remarkable classical structure, built around an octagonal rotunda in the typical fashion of the mid-19th century, is one of the largest plantations of the pre-Civil War South. The spectacular exterior of the house is matched by its interior decorations and artifices; also features gardens and orchards.

Corinth

Battery Robinette: The site of the two-day Battle of Corinth in May 1862. *Corinth Museum* also commemorates the battle, in which the Southerners deceived the Federals into thinking their evacuation trains were reinforcements and thereby managed to escape unnoticed.

Nesbit

Nesbit Ranch: Current home of rock 'n roll star Jerry Lee Lewis. This ranch, with a piano-shaped swimming pool, is open for tours, which also include the Killer Kar Museum.

Oxford

University of Mississippi; Chartered in 1844 and featuring antebellum structures, such as the **Lyceum**, the **Barnard Observatory**, and the **Old Chapel**, the university also houses the **Mississippi Blues Archive** and many museums. **Rowan Oak**, the home of author William Faulkner, is also owned by the university. The simple planter's house still contains Faulkner's typewriter, and his novel *A Fable* is outlined on the walls of his office.

Tupelo

Tupelo National Battlefield: This one-acre battlefield commemorates a battle between Lt. Gen. Nathan Bedford Forrest and Gen. A. J. Smith, who was sent to stop Forrest from destroying the Unionists' rail supply. The site is part of the **Natchez Trace Parkway.**

Elvis Presley Center: In celebration of the musical legend and the "King of Rock," this center, situated in Elvis's birth town, contains the **Elvis Presley Birthplace**, a humble two-room house that has been restored to the way it looked before Elvis moved to Memphis; the **Elvis Presley Museum**; the **Memorial Chapel**; and the **Elvis Presley Park** with recreation facilities.

MISSISSIPPI: THE SOUTHWEST

Grand Gulf

Grand Gulf Military Monument Park: Commemorates the remains of Grand Gulf town and battle site, where General Grant landed with his army in 1863. The park features original Civil War memorabilia and replicas of stockades and observation towers, as well as a 1768 **dogtrot house**, the Carpenter Gothic **Sacred Heart Catholic Church**, and a **museum** displaying Native American and Civil War artifacts.

Jackson

Mississippi State Capitol: A Beaux-Arts structure, which in 1903 replaced the old less ornate capitol building. Both guided and self-guided tours are available.

Natchez

Grand Village of the Natchez Indians: Archaeological site featuring the original earth mounds and plazas of the oldest permanent settlement on the Mississippi River. A Natchez house and corn granary have also been reconstructed on the site, and there is a museum with Native American artifacts and exhibitions on everyday life in the village.

Natchez Trace Parkway A historic 8,000-year-old trail running 500 miles through the wilderness between Natchez and Nashville. Sights along the now paved trace include the 1820s inn **Mount Locust**, a phosphate mine, an ironworks, a tobacco farm, a ferry crossing, and a Confederate grave site; *See also Natchez Trace Parkway, Central Tennessee.*

Stanton Hall: This imposing palatial mansion with its lavish and opulent decorations was built by Frederick Stanton, who imported expensive materials and ornaments for its decoration from overseas. The mansion is now open to the public.

Longwood One of the most interesting houses in America, Longwood is also the largest and most elaborate octagonal house. It now stands as an empty shell, since construction was halted during the Civil War and the interior never finished.

Port Gibson

Windsor Ruins: Only 23 ghostly Corinthian columns are left of the once opulent antebellum plantation house. An American treasure, Windsor Ruins now evoke the grand existence of the southern planters.

Vicksburg

Vicksburg National Military Park: This park is the site of Unionist General Grant's 47-day siege in 1863, which subsequently won him Vicksburg and thus the Mississippi River. A road takes visitors 16 miles through the rolling hills of the park and passes various monuments, artifacts, fortifications, and trenches. The park also hosts separate cemeteries for the Confederate and Union soldiers, as well as a visitor center.

Woodville

Rosemont: The childhood home of Jefferson Davis, this modest but beautiful planter's cottage was built in 1810. Most of the present furnishings are either original or were added by members of the five generations of the Davis family that resided in the cottage.

MISSISSIPPI: THE COAST

Biloxi

Beauvoir Jefferson Davis Home and Presidential Library: Once the home of former Confederate President Jefferson Davis, Beauvoir is named for its beautiful view of the Gulf of Mexico. Today, many of the Davis family's original possessions are still displayed in the house, and the basement hosts a museum with many items from Davis' political life. Another museum has artifacts from the war.

West Ship Island

Fort Massachusetts: The building of this fort commenced in 1857, though it was not completed until after the Civil War. Visitors can tour the fort, which is in excellent condition and houses one of the few 15-inch Roman guns left in America.